You Selfish Bastard

A Self-Help Book

by

D. Arthur Wilson

For permission, serialization, condensation, adaptations, or for our catalog of other publications, write to Ozark Mountain Publishing, Inc., P.O. Box 754, Huntsville, AR 72740, ATTN: Permissions Department.

Library of Congress Cataloging-in-Publication Data

You Selfish Bastard: A Self-Help Book
by D. Arthur Wilson -1958-

A humorous and light-hearted book hitting hard at truths about ourselves, our relationships and ultimately, our deep inner calling towards something greater than ourselves.

1. Selfish 2. Self-Care 3. Self-Help
I. Wilson, D. Arthur-1958- II. Selfish III. Self-Help IV. Title
Library of Congress Catalog Card Number: 2023930837
ISBN: 978-1-956945-35-5

Cover Art and Layout: Victoria Cooper Art
Book set in: Times New Roman and Franklin Gothic Heavy
Book Design: Summer Garr
Published by:

PO Box 754, Huntsville, AR 72740
800-935-0045 or 479-738-2348; fax 479-738-2448
WWW.OZARKMT.COM

Printed in the United States of America

Contents

Preface

I am that I am.—Popeye

You Selfish Bastard? Really? Now, I'm not a sexist, but I am a male, and that is the only reason I used that noun. If you wish, I could just as easily call this book *You Selfish Bitch*, which actually sounds very sexist. Before you get your panties in a wad, I want to let you know this book really isn't about YOU, but it may very well be. If you are reading this book, the title obviously grabbed your attention—probably a good indicator that the latter may be true.

This book is actually about me. Yes, I am a selfish bastard. The kick is, I don't want to be. To be perfectly honest, I'm not sure that I can escape this unpleasant reality, at least not completely. However, this book is not a derogatory treatise of self-abasement but rather a tale of one man embracing his own humanness all the while searching to become the man he'd like to be. It is meant to be a humorous and lighthearted search for enlightenment, or rather, a book about how to lighten up. And maybe, just maybe, there may be more to this quest than meets the eye as we traverse the happy road of pure motives and unselfish acts.

All of this leads me to a very important question: can a person ever really be totally unselfish? Before you answer too quickly, let me remind you that every person you or I have ever heard of who even hinted at being totally selfless or piously claimed to be turned out to be completely BONKERS! You know it and I know it. And if you end up believing the altruistic claims of these superhumans, then you're BONKERS too! It's like the person bragging they are the humblest—BONKERS!

There I go again; maybe offending you twice and I'm barely past the first page. I'm sure you may have thought of a few great examples of unselfishness—Jesus, Buddha, Mohammad, Moses, Krishna, Gandhi, and even Mother Theresa—but I would bet my bottom dollar that none of these men and women would claim this about themselves. However, their unselfishness was definitely touted by their followers.

I believe all of these great leaders would humbly describe themselves in the simplest of terms and boast not of their great, inspiring deeds of selflessness. So I stand by my original statement that anyone claiming to be totally unselfish is totally BONKERS! Which leads me to this question: what exactly is *selfish* by definition? Here is what Webster has to say:

> **selfish**
> **adjective**
> self·ish | \ 'sel-fish \
> **Definition of *selfish***
> **1:** concerned excessively or exclusively with oneself: seeking or concentrating on one's own advantage, pleasure, or well-being without regard for others.

This definition leads me to a few additional questions. Who defines the relative term *excessive*? Is there a unified scale we can all agree upon, or is this completely arbitrary? Is it judged by others or by ourselves? Who decides?

By all outward appearances, it would appear to be a judgment used almost exclusively about others and rarely if ever about ourselves. We are very good at, and quick for that matter, to notice acts of selfishness in our fellows, but can we honestly say that we frequently notice our own selfishness? Speaking for myself, I usually have very good reasons for my own selfishness, if I even call it that. Interesting, yes?

Included in this definition is that a selfish person is only thinking of himself or herself. Does this mean if I think of others too—that is, as well as myself—I'm no longer selfish? Do I get the proverbial "get out of jail free card" from the prison for selfish bastards and the like?

Finally, what if I am not thinking about pleasure or advantage but disadvantage, like all the terrible stuff I've done or that has been done to me? What if I am completely consumed with me and all the past wrongs perpetrated to me and by me? What if I can't think about anybody else because I'm riveted on me and how terribly I have been treated or have treated others? Am I left begging for mercy on the steps of the high courts by judges who would heap ever more vengeance upon my already ravaged soul? Is it selfish to be concerned with only myself and these wrongdoings? What then? Maybe I need more than just a definition of the word *selfish*. Maybe I need some synonyms too.

Here's what Webster has to say about that:

Synonyms for *selfish*

Synonyms

- egocentric
- egoistic
- egomaniacal
- egotistical
- narcissistic
- self-absorbed
- self-centered
- self-concerned
- self-infatuated
- self-involved
- self-obsessed
- self-preoccupied
- self-seeking
- self-serving

Well, there you have it! Does that help? Not sure?

Then again, looking at the list of synonyms, can anyone really be free from egotism, narcissism, and self-centeredness? Isn't the very act of declaring yourself free from these bedevilments egotistic at its core? A person must think very highly of himself or herself even to try and make such a statement.

So now my question is this. Isn't this entire process of determining whether I am a selfish person simply an effort to find out how I am perceived by another? It really has little to do with whether I am actually selfish, but rather if I am being judged to be. In other words, how do I stack up to my fellows? Wouldn't all the concern about how I measure up be very similar to self-obsession and worrying about what other people think of me? However, if I don't consider others' feelings about my actions, then I am definitely selfish, right?

I'm confused! I mean, really confused! If a person was truly selfless and unselfish, would he or she even be asking these questions? Maybe if we stop right here, we can avoid this awkward questioning and assume that we are indeed UNSELFISH.

Ha! Wouldn't you just love that? Me too!

But, if you're like most people, you want to know if you are selfish or not, or, possibly, the right degree of selfishness and selflessness. It's obvious that we care what other people think.

Nothing self-centered about that!

And what about that rule on the airplane? The one where if the oxygen masks drop, you put your mask on first before helping the person beside you? Is that selfish? To help yourself so you can help others? There must be an answer. That is why I'm writing this book. Perhaps together we can find an answer and a way to live happily with the answer we find.

Chapter One

In the Beginning …
There was COVID-19

Every story has a beginning (my beginning started sixty-three years ago); however, I am going to start this story in April 2020, in the middle of the COVID-19 crisis gripping the world in its huge but microscopically small fearful teeth. I am also typing this with one hand as I just blew out my collarbone mountain biking last Friday.

It's slow going, to say the least. But here I am. My career as an artist has been temporarily suspended by the injury, and I have been left with nothing but time on my hands. I've watched about as much Netflix as I can stand, and I am feeling the incredible itch to do something productive. Something worthwhile! Something that would help people! Something that would help me!

During a meditation, as I pondered my great purpose, this title flashed before my eyes: *You Selfish Bastard*. I saw the entire book, with a white cover and the title in bold red letters, as it sat on a shelf in the Self-Help section of Barnes & Noble. It was a VISION! The idea of seeing this title among the other serious titles made me laugh hard, and I knew immediately I had to write this book and this book was meant for me. Now you and, hopefully, many others might get something out of this, but I assure you, this book is definitely written about me, to me, and for me! You are conveniently let off the hook, so to speak. That's only if you want to be.

So here I am during the COVID-19 apocalypse, and every day I am hearing about another wonderful act someone is performing during this worldwide catastrophe. People are taking food to others, volunteering, performing free concerts online, singing together, praying for one another. I am truly taken aback by how selfless and loving so many people on this planet really are, and just how giving. This is the driving force behind this book. I'm watching wonderful things happen all around me. I watch the people doing them and I marvel, first at them, but then at myself. I marvel that I don't seem to think the same way they do. Am I missing something here? What these people are doing doesn't even occur to me to do—well, maybe after they've already done it, sure, but everybody does that! No, I can safely say it's rarely my first thought—thinking of others. But somehow these people do!

All of this raises another question: what do these incredible angels of mercy have that I don't? Did they learn to be that way? Were they born that way? Raised that way? How did they get that way? And how do I get that way too? There I go being selfish again!

You've heard many people say, "a leopard doesn't change its spots" or "people never change." If that's true, then these people, these angels of benevolent love, must have been born that way and I might as well give up now. I mean, what's the use? What's my use, if that's really true? Are they just born that way and the rest of us aren't? Are they just lucky, blessed, fortunate, gifted, and all-around better people than we are? Does this mean we are just left out, DOOMED to eke out a life of selfish pursuits and lonely acquisition? Are we destined to a meaningless, unhappy end? Could that be true? To make matters worse, those goody two-shoes appear to be happy, very HAPPY! So here we are, the selfish bitches and bastards of the world, and we must just accept our lot in life if it is indeed true that they are just lucky or born that way.

But does any one of us actually believe that? And if we do, what does that say about us? I'll tell you what it says about us: not only are we selfish, we're victims too! Which is short for "it's everybody else's fault." But we'll deal with victims in a later chapter. Where was I?

Back to my story. We are in this worldwide crisis and the best is coming out in many of those around me and the worst in a few. What is so beautiful to me during this time is the appearance of a choice. Which do *I* want to be? Selfish or unselfish? Happy or unhappy? Blessed or cursed? Lucky or unlucky? Loved or unloved? Loving or unloving?

So, assuming we've decided to believe we actually do have a choice, and that that choice is to be happily unselfish, then it is obvious that it's not going to just happen. If that were the case, it already would have happened, and we would now be one of those people everybody is reading about or watching on Facebook, Instagram, or YouTube being all lovey and sweet and giving and just incredibly WONDERFUL! We would be one of THEM. The LUCKY GOODY FREAKIN' TWO-SHOES!

Instead, I am writing a book titled *You Selfish Bastard* in the hope of finding my way through the fog of self-centered egotism and stepping confidently ashore at last upon the white sands of selflessness and true love and compassion for my fellow man. That is, of course, if the anchor of self-justification tied at my waist doesn't drown me first. What do I mean by that? I think we are ready for chapter 2.

Chapter Two

SELF-ish

To thine own self be true.—Shakespeare

It may seem paradoxical to suggest the way to freedom from selfishness is through the journey into self, but I am suggesting exactly that. Shakespeare's famous quote has been so widely repeated throughout the years that virtually no one hasn't heard it. In fact, we celebrate it frequently and use it at will, predominantly as a license to "be ourselves." And many times, we use it as a justification for all kinds of thinly veiled selfish behavior.

I know I've done it!

But here, the word *selfish* is not to be confused with *self-ish*, even though the two may look identical. Here, I use *self-ish* like we use the words *pinkish* or *bluish*, describing a hue or hint of a particular color but not completely pink or blue. This is precisely the way I would suggest we look at our SELVES. Our true SELVES. How close are we to our true color? Our true nature? WHO we truly are? Are we just a hint or a resemblance of our true color? Or maybe we show up as a completely different color altogether. Do you get my drift?

I'm an artist by trade and have been making a living selling my paintings since 1978. Art means a great deal to me, so I will use many metaphors about paint, light, shading, etc. It is in my bones to think this way. I remember when I started making my living painting and selling art; I had just finished a pen-and-ink

4

outline of a raccoon hanging on a branch. I painstakingly drew every hair of that creature with a 0 aught quill pen (which is very, very small), dipping the pen in my indigo inkwell every two or three strokes. I was very proud of my painting and very proud of all the detail work I had done.

Now I wanted to attempt something I had never tried before. I was going to add color with watercolor washes—that is, several thin washes of color laid over the black-and-white image with just a hint of color again and again. Having never done this before, I cautiously and lightly painted the background. I then brought blues and browns and tan and pink onto the body of the raccoon. It was looking awesome! It had been easy and quick, as if the painting was painting itself. Magic!

Then came the ever-so-familiar thought of self-doubt, the voice of reason. "It can't be that easy. I haven't worked long enough or hard enough on this piece." This was self-doubt, the ever-present and necessary companion of every great artist, painter, or performer. Without some form of self-doubt, we artists are void of the drive necessary to push always forward. It is an artist's greatest gift and greatest failing.

Instead of trusting my own eyes or my newly formed artistic instinct, my old work ethic won the day and I started adding more colors, working harder and harder. Needless to say, the painting became darker and darker, muddier and muddier, with each new layer. Before long, the painting no longer resembled the light and beautiful piece I had had just half an hour before. Now the entire thing was one big, brown, blurry mess. The beautiful pen-and-ink sketch, buried under layer after layer of watercolor, had become virtually invisible. I had destroyed the painting by overworking it. I hated it now and I had loved it only moments earlier. I have never forgotten that lesson.

Examining yourself for the first time might be exactly like this. Perhaps you liked what you saw a while back or when you were young, or maybe you had never liked what you had created. The point is, looking into yourself through critical eyes will tend to overwork an otherwise beautiful thing and will most surely destroy the beauty of this experience. So be easy on yourself. Don't look so hard that you muddy the canvas of your life and it becomes darker and darker. Just make your start. Keep it light, like watercolor washes. Pull out a blank canvas if you need to.

You can do that, you know. You don't have to just paint over the old one again and again. You can start anew—today. REALLY!

Today can mark the beginning of your quest, or, rather, your question, if you will, the beginning of a lifelong journey toward a destination full of promise and value, a quest packed to the brim with the richest and finest things this life has to offer, one which provides relief from the bondage of selfishness as you enter a new freedom of knowing exactly who and what you are. As you venture forward, you will gain an ever-clearer vision of purpose and deep fulfillment. What is this quest or rather, question?

"Who the hell are you?" Helluva question, isn't it?

Do yourself a favor and really think upon this question. To answer too quickly or to brush lightly over the top of this question would be unfortunate. It would be like running over the grass with your lawn mower set too high. Just as with the mower, you might end up making a lot of noise and spending a lot of time mowing, but you're just not going to get the job done. You need to cut low enough but not too low as to kill the grass. (I spent a lot of summers mowing the yard.)

So how do I know if I have set my depth to the right level? There is a word, an awesome word, a word that isn't used much anymore but it's one of my favorite words in the English language. It describes a simple approach when considering a new idea or concept. It's a word that when applied will help us get to the bottom of things. There's a peace about this word, and it implies a lack of strenuous effort. It's a relaxing word. It's a word of profound importance. It's a word that will help in not overworking the canvas of your life.

The word is *ponder*. If you can honestly commit to truly ponder your quest, your question, then I would personally guarantee that you could put this book down and you would never again be the same. Once you start asking the RIGHT questions, pondering their meanings, the universe can't help but respond and take hold of you and never, ever let you go. This reminds me of a few phrases I have come to know and trust as absolute, universal truths.

Seek and you shall find.

Knock and the door shall open to you.

And ...

The truth shall set you FREE!

You might be thinking that I missed one. That one is "Ask and it shall be given unto you." But that is for another chapter.

Remember, don't just skim lightly over this question. Let it sink in. Ponder! What does *ponder* really mean? Here's what Webster has to say about it:\

Ponder
<u>verb</u>
pon·der | \ 'pän-dər \
pondered; pondering\ 'pän-d(ə-)riŋ \
Definition of *ponder*
<u>transitive verb</u>
1: to weigh in the mind : APPRAISE *pondered* their chances of success
2: to think about : reflect on *pondered* the events of the day
<u>intransitive verb</u>
: to think or consider especially quietly, soberly and deeply

I think I like the last one best—to think or consider quietly, soberly, and deeply. While you're pondering, this may be a good time to explain a little more about this book you're holding in your hands. When we contemplate ourselves and the world about us, we examine the obvious and the not so obvious, the seen and the unseen, the known and the unknown. There will be many opportunities for AHA moments. There will also be mention of mysterious things, mystical and magical. There are many words to describe these events and the power that animates them. Some of these terms you may take issue with. I will do my best not to arouse any prejudice, but I will ask you, the reader, to please translate any possibly offensive term into a language that resonates with you personally, for you don't want to miss the forest for the trees, so to speak. Along this path of discovery, there will be mentioned forces at work, an invisible power available to us all. There will be mention of the universe, God and creative intelligence, and any number of descriptions to try and convey the spiritual side of life. It would seem near to impossible not to offend someone with one of these phrases, but I would hate that you miss the point all because a particular noun was used instead of another. I am not here to sell you on any particular faith or path. I am just here to help you on yours. I will leave you to ponder now.

Chapter Three
Still Here?

Where?

You're still HERE?

I'm glad! Most of us humanoids need more than a little help while navigating this thing we call life. How does this pertain to selfishness? Life as we know it is only seen through the eyes of the self, and since the self is where selfishness originates, nothing could hold more value than a thorough searching of the self and the discovering of our true nature.

Have you had time to ponder? Or did you just turn the page and decide to keep reading, saving pondering for later? In any case, I think it is important to reiterate, in as much benefit that can be derived by others, I can assure you, this book has definitely benefited me. For after all, it is for me, to me, and about me. But because you are still here and along for the ride, I should probably spell out some of the things I have found along the way. I will endeavor to describe how I began my own journey of discovering WHO I really am.

You may be wondering why I asked you WHERE you are at the top of this chapter, and you may even wonder WHAT that could possibly have to do with WHO you are. It has everything to do with WHO you are and everything else too! It also has much to do with WHEN. And the answer is right in front of your nose.

It is very important to notice WHERE your feet are and not where your head is. We all know our feet can be one place and our thoughts miles away. Lifetimes away! We can be thinking about things past, sometimes far past, and like we were time traveling at the speed of light, we can be immediately rocketed into the future. Often one element of time is filled with feelings of remorse, guilt, shame, or some other form of regret, and the other is filled with uncertainty, doubt, fear, and maybe even an overwhelming sense of dread or doom, always waiting for the proverbial other shoe to drop. I am sure you can guess which is which, which is past and which is future. How do I know this? I have spent much of my life existing between these two extremes and rarely exactly WHERE my feet are. But YOU don't have to! I want you to read the next three paragraphs very slowly and try to really digest their true meaning.

You can choose to start right here in this most perfect of all places—the HERE and NOW. Notice it is the WHERE and the WHEN, and they are very much the same, one and the other. Space and time, it would appear, in this setting, are identical, indistinguishable, and inseparable. It must be here and now because you cannot be here and then, for you would really not be here anymore, if it was then. You would be then and there! Likewise, you cannot be there and now, can you? Being anywhere other than here, we cannot experience now, now can we? No, you must be here in order to experience now and vice versa. Interesting!

You could try to start from the past or the future and let me know how that works out for you. But HERE is WHERE all the magic happens, and NOWHERE else. Anything other than HERE is nowhere. There is nowhere else you can actually start from. Nothing, absolutely NO THING exists outside of this present moment, except maybe our thoughts about something existing in the past or future, but even that thought is happening NOW.

When you are stuck in your thoughts, either past or future, know you are stuck in the imaginary world of nowhere, a place that actually doesn't even exist. It is hard to get your mind around that, isn't it? But life is happening NOW, and only now. To live anywhere other than now is to not be living at all. Not really.

Another way to break down or look at the word *nowhere* is NOW HERE, the opposite of *nowhere*. You have probably heard this before, and, as with most clichés, it may have run its course. You may even think it is cute as its importance gently slips right by you. But I would be remiss if I were to gloss over this extremely profound starting point in anyone's journey. To not contemplate (ponder) this thought, this idea of the present NOW, and find the absolute marvel of the moment, to relish in this simple awareness and to find the profundity of it would be as absurd as going to watch the sunset on the beach and facing east. You're there but you're missing all the action.

What does it mean to be present? How do we get there? How do we get HERE?

We're already there. I mean here.

"This is going to be hard," you might be thinking. Well, it might be hard or it might be easy, and it all depends on what you want it to be. Yes, it depends on you! You can label it as hard and I assure you it will be very difficult to get into the moment, but you can just as easily make it EASY. That's funny! "You can just as EASILY make it EASY!" Sometimes the cleverest things come out of my mouth. Does that ever happen to you? You're just rambling along and something wise, poignant, or profound comes sailing past your lips? When this happens, it makes me wonder WHERE thoughts actually come from. Do you ever think about that? If a thought was never in your brain to begin with, and nobody told you this particular thought, and, suddenly, like magic, a new thought appears out of thin air, where does that thought come from? Mysterious! Anyway, where was I? Oh yeah, I was about to tell you, you can make it hard or easy and it really doesn't matter. What matters is simply that you DO it! "Do what?" you ask.

NOTHING.

That's right! I want you to do nothing. NO THING.

Well, except for one thing, which really is something.

PONDER.

"Ponder what?"

Nothing.

Except maybe one thing ...

NOW.

Seriously! I want you to ponder NOW, now!

You can approach pondering any way you like. Pondering is not really trying to answer a question but rather sitting quietly in the midst of the question and allowing those mysterious thoughts you have never thought before just simply come to you, through you, for you, floating down from the ether like mysterious greeting cards arriving by airmail or email, sender unknown.

You would probably much rather DO something, anything other than nothing, but you simply can't get THERE until you do.

WHERE?

HERE.

NOW.

SERIOUSLY!

If I could ponder for you, I would. This is something you must do for yourself. Sit quietly and just let the moment at hand come and go, blending gently and seamlessly into the next. Empty your mind of all future thoughts and any past ones as well. Allow your awareness to expand, taking in this present moment in its entirety, the sounds, the sights, the smells. What are you experiencing? Really look, really hear, really smell, touch, and taste. Immerse yourself in NOW! Stay there/here as long as possible and ponder.

Chapter Four
Lost & Found

Now, I'm not psychic (actually, we all are a little), but I'm guessing you could be feeling a little lost right now. You might be thinking, "D. Arthur, I thought you were going to tell us about your path through selfishness and self-centeredness to selflessness and compassion for our fellow man, and instead you leave us to ponder the moment, time/space, and where our feet are, and what does that have to do with the price of tea in China?"

Wow! That is an old saying! "What does that have to do with the price of tea in China?" Really old! I haven't heard that phrase for more than half a century. And now it's coming out of my own mouth. If you will bear with me, I am sure you will eventually discover for yourself how and why all of this is attached to selfishness as well as selflessness. I am just setting the tone, setting the stage. The play is about to begin. My truest desire is that you end up finding your own path, your own answers, and your own relationship with this divine mystery we call life. You are the star of the show.

We are all on our own unique path, and no one else can walk your path or in your shoes. Truth be told, no one else really wants to, and if you can get very, very honest with yourself, neither would you. I mean, if you could walk someone else's path or your own, guaranteed, you'd pick your own every time. Sure, you might wish your path was a little clearer or less filled with thorns and underbrush and maybe with a few more dollars in the bank, but given the choice between living your life or living someone else's, you'd pick yours.

Why? Because your story is still the most fascinating thing in your life and you know it! It has held your attention since the day you were born. That is the way it's supposed to be. It is your favorite story and it's the only story you have—the story of YOU. It's also the story of ME, if you know what I mean. A riveting tale of woe and tragedy, trials and triumphs. Yes, your story is totally fascinating and YOU are its author and you are the principal character. You are writing your novel; you are writing your life as you go along. And as with every great story, it should have a happy ending. It's up to you alone whether you have a happy ending or not. Everybody loves a happy ending. This is one of the reasons I'm writing this book. I want my happy ending too! Lord knows I've created enough drama for a good story line. For your amusement, here's a little story from the book of ME, D. Arthur.

I had been a freelance artist for twenty years. I had made a living, purchased three modest homes, and supported my first wife and my son solely by the sales of my art, an accomplishment in and of itself. I was represented by as many as forty galleries scattered throughout the United States and even had a gallery representing my work in Switzerland. I was noted in *US Art*, *Wildlife Art News*, *Southwest Art Magazine*, and *Art Business News*, and I also garnered an acknowledgment in *Who's Who in America*. I was making a living, but just barely. My father liked to remind me of that and the fact that I was living under the poverty level, even though I didn't feel like it. But he would remind me nonetheless. I think it was mostly because no parent likes to watch their child suffer, whether by someone else's hand or their own.

So, there I was, forty years old, recently divorced and barely eking out a living when I met and married my second wife, Lisa. There are a few things to know about Lisa. I had come from a family of seven children, and Lisa was an only child. I had a definite artistic leaning toward the liberal, and Lisa was a Dallas gal with a definite leaning toward the conservative. I was raised poor, and Lisa was raised with a silver spoon in her mouth. Literally! In fact, I was just informed that it is a tradition in her family—and now in our family—to give the newborns not only a silver spoon but a silver cup as well. We have four grandbabies now, and they all have their own silver spoons and cups. It's a thing, I guess. I didn't know! I was raised with a Dixie cup and a spork.

I guess you could say my wife and I are opposites, and you would be mostly right. Most people would also agree that I married up. They, especially the men, like to remind me of this, as I married a real looker. She is a stunningly beautiful mother of three, and I must keep her somewhat entertained, as we will be celebrating twenty years of marital bliss next month as I write this. The point of this story is this: I was a struggling artist barely surviving with an ex-wife and one son, and I married up to a woman with three of her own growing, very active, teenaged, hungry young men.

I cannot tell you the terror I felt when, seemingly overnight, I went from feeding three mouths to six: four growing boys with huge appetites, my new gorgeous wife, and myself. By the way, gorgeous costs! Don't let anyone tell you differently. So there I was. My responsibilities had more than doubled, but my income had stayed the same. And there would be silver cups and spoons in my future too. What to do?

This added pressure created necessary weight, not unlike the enormous, crushing weight a diamond must feel in order to be formed. This added pressure was the required ingredient to create something completely new in my life, and it would soon transform my life forever. It would appear that the old adage that "necessity is the mother of all invention" is correct.

Enter Rhupert!

Yes, Rhupert! My bird brainchild, an iconic ostrich art form with a paradoxical message based on a quote from Oscar Wilde: "Life is too important to be taken seriously." Rhupert's message, boiled down, is to simply be yourself. I use Rhupert to convey this message and to deliver it under the guise of humor. If you simply search the internet for Rhupert the ostrich, you'll see what I mean.

Not only did Rhupert's message transform my life, it also transformed my career. When I jumped ship from my established wildlife art career and bet it all on my new creation, I had no idea what was to follow. First, all of the galleries I had worked with for years suddenly dropped my work completely and stated emphatically in reference to Rhupert, "We can't sell this!" I was now stuck between a rock and a hard place—no galleries to sell my work and yet a burning knowledge in my gut that I really had something new and fresh, and besides, the world needed Rhupert!

In a last-ditch effort and after a great deal of pondering, my wife and I decided to do something different. We were going to open our own gallery in Key West, Florida, right in the center of Duval Street. Duval Street is a super busy, bustling street in a bustling tourist island town. Think Las Vegas meets Laguna Beach. This was not going to be an easy task as I had a grand total of $500 in the bank and I had no idea how we were going to come up with the necessary $100,000 to pull this off. I just knew we were going to do it. Besides, I had already pondered for a long time. It was time now for action.

Well, needless to say, the money mysteriously showed up (a story in itself), and off we went in a big, shiny U-Haul to sunny Key West, Florida. It was the biggest gamble of my career but soon would prove the wisest decision I could have ever made. Rhupert went on to sell like hotcakes—like hotcakes were ever a big seller. But just as that colloquialism implies, Rhupert went on to gain many new galleries and to pick up collectors in all fifty states and more than twenty-five countries worldwide. Singlehandedly, Rhupert, my wacky bird-brained messenger, transformed me, my career, and my finances forever.

Rhupert had taught me again the lesson of following one's heart. Over the years, Rhupert has gone on to say many other truths about life and this comical quest we are all on. One of my all-time favorite quotes I attribute to Rhupert is the following: "There are three things in life most difficult to do. The first is to find out WHO you are. The second is to BE who you are. And the third and most scary thing in life to do is this: To SHARE who you really are!"

It takes immense courage to launch out on the never-ending journey to FIND YOURSELF, BE YOURSELF, and SHARE YOURSELF. Yet there is no higher calling, no greater purpose, and no more thrilling ride. This is YOUR life. YOUR story. Make it a good one. Make it pleasing to yourself. Is that selfish? Maybe. Maybe not.

There is one thing I have also learned on this journey of self-discovery. You must do this part alone. Nobody else has the expertise to work it out for you. You are the world's leading authority on YOU. In fact, you have your PhD on the subject:

your Profound honest Discovery of yourself. I cannot motivate you; that is your job. I cannot drive your desires or give you the necessary commitment to do what comes in the next chapters. But I can *INSPIRE* you to seek, to knock, and to trust that your heart will lead you where you need to go. I can also invite you to take a leap of faith, to believe that an extraordinary idea just may exist outside of your previous thought and that it may be what you've been looking for all along. Remember, seek and ye shall find, knock and the door shall be open to you, and the truth shall set you free.

Chapter Five
This Is Not SELF-Help

I was raised by a thinker to be a thinker, and it was my job in life to figure things out, to think. So you can imagine my dismay that when it came to figuring out how to be happy and to have true love and compassion for my fellow man, I was at a complete loss. It did not come naturally to me. To make matters worse, it seemed the harder I tried, the less happy I was and the greater my obsession with "me" became. This thing called life appeared to be a conundrum and beyond my ability to make any lasting progress in attaining selflessness and/or happiness.

It became apparent that if I was to figure this thing out, I was going to need help and a lot of it. Many of us tried to operate upon the principles we were taught as children, but the idea that I, in and of myself, must hold all the answers as an adult, soon proved pure folly. Truth was, if I had the answers I was seeking, I would no longer be seeking, yes? I would already be so loving and wonderful you just wouldn't be able to stand me. But here I sat at the end of my own resourcefulness, left wanting.

That is why I say this is not self-help. It is my strong belief that no man is an island and we all must have a little help now and again. Emphasis on "again." Needing help, it turns out, was not a sign of weakness but strength, orchestrated in a grand design by a loving universe.

Seeking help outside ourselves is actually an intrinsic part of our quest for strength, happiness, and love. Our *need* is our gift to others. Read that again. Our need is our gift. Yes, our NEED is our GIFT!

How can that be? you might ask. Here's the skinny on that: when we *need*, we allow others to step up and become who they really want to be—loving, caring, and selfless. It is a symbiotic relationship between giver and recipient. Without someone in need, there is no opportunity to give and thus no opportunity to feel compassion, to BE unselfish.

At that particular point in my life, it was my turn to be needy and I did not care for it, not one little bit! I know how this may sound—me having to receive help, it felt awful and oh, how I wanted to always be the giver, the one helping, the voice of hope, ABOVE it all, BETTER than. I wanted to have it all together, always! Quite egotistical of me, wouldn't you say? Insisting to always be the giver and never the give-ee?

Living in this manner is much like sitting in the audience at an opera and demanding to be on the stage, or finally getting to be on stage and with the spotlight shining ever so brightly on me, demanding never to sit in an audience again. However, if we spend time solely on the stage or solely in the audience, we then rob ourselves of a much greater experience.

To not only watch the spectacle but to be the spectacle. Both are equally important experiences.

For the play to be a success, there must be the audience and the performers—the givers and the receivers. And if there is no audience, that is called a dress rehearsal, and in LIFE, there are no dress rehearsals.

I was at a place in life where in order to find peace, love, and happiness, and my purpose, I was going to have to reach out and ask for help FIRST. I hated it! And by a series of unfortunate, I mean, fortunate, events, I found myself in just such a place where I absolutely had to ask for help if I was to turn my life around.

I needed a thought, guidance that was obviously outside of me. As a man who prided myself on being a lone wolf, this was a crushing blow to my ego. But it was a necessary one. In fact, I believe there is no greater foe than one's own ego. I have since learned a great motto: "my ego is not my amigo." Everybody's got an ego, as it turns out. It may lean to grandiosity in our positive traits or grandiosity in our negative ones. Or both. Either way, our egos are not here to assist in balancing themselves. Our egos quite often make a complete mess of our lives, our relationships, and ultimately how we see ourselves. Our egos will fight to the bitter end to defend their sense of self, and from the ego's death-defying stance stems every act of cruelty and selfishness.

All of this raises another question: does the ego reflect the true YOU? The true ME? Is that WHO we really are, just little EGOs running around shouting, "look at ME, look at ME?" For many of us, that is exactly who we are, and that is the reason for the title of this book. But before we point the proverbial finger at those obvious egos living about us, we might want to know that our own egos love nothing more than to look down from their lofty places of reverent holiness and condemn others, one and all, for their perceived faults, all the while conveniently turning a blind eye upon our own egoist misgivings. Don't do it! It's a trap! Our egos will look for any way to feel superior to our fellow travelers. And if our egos can wrap themselves in the lily-white robes of righteousness or some other great cause, all the better.

"It's just not right." "Who do they think they are?" "Why, I never." "Look how egotistical they are." "Look how selfish!" "I'm so glad I'm not like that." "I am so spiritual now; I would never do that." "Bless their hearts," you might say sweetly (masking your condemnation) under your breath so as not to sound arrogant. If you've ever thought or said any of these things, then GOOD! You have now admitted you have an ego. This is the first step to enlightenment. But the truth is, you always have and you always will have an ego. And it's also this very truth that shall set you FREE! Very dangerous indeed are the persons claiming to be above the need for an EGO. They are truly the unfortunate ones as they have found a way to believe their own deceptions, and soon their egos will set out on the grand task of convincing every ego within earshot of their newfound victory over this deadly foe. The ego is like the thief who steals your wallet and then helps you look for it. SLY DEVIL! But do not be discouraged, for it is my contention that we have an ego for a reason. A fundamental need. Otherwise, we wouldn't have it, now would we?

Before we can figure out what that need may be, we might want to figure out what the EGO really IS. This must be approached with extreme caution as we can very easily slip upon the slippery slope of spiritual competitiveness. Now, I may not know exactly what the ego is scientifically, but I do know what mine does. I know my ego loves to be *better than* or *worse than* others, on top of the heap or underneath it (two sides of the same coin). I also know my EGO is always trying to separate me out of the herd, place me as somehow weirder than everybody else, and that it loves to focus on my differences instead of my similarities. I know my EGO loves to judge others and myself. In fact, this is what it does best—JUDGE! And right along with that, my EGO LOVES, LOVES, LOVES being RIGHT! "I HATE judgmental people, and I LOVE to judge judgmental people," my ego shouts rather erroneously. My ego is also very, very CLEVER.

So, if we must all have egos and there's really no escaping them and they cause us such tremendous pain and suffering, then what could possibly be the reason for having these egos in the first place? I am not a psychologist or a psychiatrist, but I do have an ego, and since my discovery and acute awareness of this ornery live-in companion, I have come to know him quite well and have figured out a few things about him.

My ego is like an overbearing and controlling family member who lives with me 24/7. He's like a twin, or, rather, a Siamese twin, connected at the waist. He looks like me, talks like me, and even acts like me, but that is where the similarity ends. My evil twin is persistent, persuasive, and very convincing in his arguments. He is totally committed to his belief that he is always right. And he 100% sure, at all times, that he knows what's best for me. He is absolutely relentless as he tries to manipulate me to do his bidding. My twin is ruled by fear and logic, and it's his logic that usually wins me over to his way of thinking.

He is fearful of either not getting something he wants or losing something he already has. That includes mental concepts as well, especially when it concerns his/my rights. My twin is very, very moral and this is the one that trips me up the most. If my ego can convince me that not only am I right, but that it's my moral obligation to do something about it, then I can justify just about any abhorrent behavior. I know I am not the only one with such a relationship with the ego.

The question isn't how to get rid of my pesky twin (killing my Siamese twin will kill me in the process), but rather how to find a place of neutrality, a place of safety or peace, like when two warring nations agree to a PEACE TREATY. We must call a truce, lay down our arms, and stop the bloodshed. We can then draw out a border and put the terms to paper. And by both parties signing the treaty, we agree never to invade or persuade the other side ever again. Then and only then can we share in peaceful trade.

Did I mention that my ego is also a LIAR and cannot be trusted? I must also protect my borders with vigilance as my ego loves to go undercover and sneak his way back into my sovereign nation. I must never forget who my ego is or what he is capable of. I cannot either escape his existence or wish him away. I'm stuck with him, just like a Siamese twin. If I forget the true nature of my neighbor, I am in trouble. If I try to change him, I am in trouble. If I judge him, I am in trouble. If I believe him, I am in trouble. My best defense is to KNOW him, yet not to listen to or believe him. Easier said than done.

Let's assume now that I KNOW him and what he is capable of. There's still the question of just what the purpose could be of such a relationship. There must be a logical explanation. Well, this is where it may get a little weird. And the answer points to the very meaning of life itself and what it is that separates us from the animals, from the single-celled amoeba to the largest creature on the planet, the blue whale.

Egos, our live-in, bad-natured twin as it would turn out, is the very ingredient/entity necessary for the propagation of free choice. Without our egos, we could not exist, at least not as we are. Without our egos, we would be no different from any other living organism on the face of the earth, for animals appear to not suffer in the least from egoist influence.

Our egos create a CHOICE. It is choice that makes us human. Real CHOICE. We cannot have good unless there is bad. We cannot have light without darkness. We cannot have right if there is no left or up if there is no down. It is our egos that allow us this choice, to choose wrongly, if you will, that separates us from the animal kingdom. No other animal can or will deliberately choose wrong. We are unique in this quality and we have the ego to thank for it.

We can also choose right. But you cannot have one without the other. The universe as we know it could not exist without CHOICE. And good and evil are just one of a trillion billion million choices out there. This is another perspective of the theory of relativity, one that, at its core, states that one only exists as it relates to its opposite. We are different from anything else in the universe, and it's our freedom of choice that makes us so. It is choice that gives us our unique perspective of ourselves and our world, and, by some theologians' viewpoints, our likeness to the creator himself. It is our ability to choose that bears a resemblance to God, and this resemblance has nothing to do with our physicality. Our egos would love to say differently, for our egos cannot imagine a likeness other than our own as God's true image.

The very thing that makes us godlike is none other than our egos at play, exercising free choice. Thus is the very real NEED for the EGO, the true unsung hero of the cosmos. Our unsightly Siamese twin, it would appear, is very important after all.

Just don't tell him that: it would most likely go to his head.

Chapter Six
Think Again!

It's not what you think. Once we've made the quantum leap in understanding that our egos are not our amigos and that we do not have to take on the ego's likeness or fear, we are now free to explore the more important question, the REAL question: "Who am I?" If the ego is not me, the real me, the authentic me, then WHO is?

Here the ego may rush in to answer, "I'm a doctor. I'm a lawyer. I'm an artist. I'm a wife. I'm a mother. I'm a Jew. I'm a Christian." Or it may answer very negatively. "I'm disgusting. I'm fat. I'm ugly. I'm a loser. I'm a failure!" Either way, don't listen to it! None of these things are really YOU. Who you are has nothing to do with what you do or how you look.

"Who are you?" is probably the biggest question you will ever face in your life, and happiness and well-being rest upon your sincere search for the answer to this question. Taking on this quest is not for sissies and it is paramount in your efficacy in unburdening yourself of the incredible weight of selfishness and egotism.

Finding yourself, the quest of self-discovery first made popular in the 1960s and revisited by every generation since, has been largely misunderstood and many times presented as the ultimate act of selfish pursuit by airy-fairy space cadet hippies. Nothing could be further from the truth. And just as popular as the finding yourself movement was the many comedians with their sarcastic comedic response. Although hilarious, their comedy was a reaction to the very vulnerable quest of discovering the authentic self. The discomfort created when facing such tough questions as "who are you?" was perpetuated by people's own insecure, fragile egos desperately trying to maintain their camouflage. Disguising their authentic selves from discovery through misdirection and distraction, these egos rally other egos to their cause in a last-ditch attempt to humiliate through peer pressure, ever bolstering their false sense of self, all the while hiding safely behind the comedic act. So widely is this act celebrated that we often label it "real," "down to earth," or even "humble." The ego is so SLY!

I have done my share of discrediting those things that I do not understand or that make me uncomfortable, and it's easy now to see why. Fear! When people are sincere and authentic, it makes those of us who are hiding very uncomfortable. "What if I am discovered?" our egos shriek in horror. And if we could get really honest and finish that sentence, it would sound something like this: "If you really knew me, you wouldn't like me."

So most of us on the face of the planet spend our lives hiding in plain sight, with very few if any of the people around us ever truly getting to know us. And the kicker is, we probably don't really know them either. Not our wives, our husbands, or even our children know us when we insist on presenting only the images our egos deemed SAFE for human relationship. If we are severely dominated by our egos, we should probably carry a bright orange warning label pasted across our hearts. WARNING! This person may have many artificial ingredients and may not be safe for human relationship! So we hide. We never really get close to anyone. We become lonely, depressed, and distrusting. Yet we probably don't have a clue why.

What is the answer? You tell me. You are the authority on YOU. It's not my job to know what's best for you! It's yours. But I can tell you what I have found out about ME and what works for me. And it starts with another story ...

I was raised, as I said before, with six siblings. It was by and large a very happy childhood with a few exceptions. Both my mom and my dad were preacher's kids, PKs as we called them in the church. They both were raised with an understandably huge dose of religious dogma and every negative thing that comes along with that. That structure also provided a very kind and loving environment at the same time. Needless to say, I was raised by two very loving parents who couldn't help but filter down these moral teachings and dogmas. Right or wrong, I was raised believing in God, Jesus, and the whole kit and caboodle.

I was raised believing that, on one hand, God is love and, on the other, he was going to strike me dead if I did anything wrong. Then there was his son, Jesus, who loved me regardless. It was God I was going to have to watch out for, but Jesus had my back. We were buds! There I was, never really questioning my faith as a youth, but as I grew older, many things just didn't seem to add up anymore. When I discussed any of these issues with my religious friends, they would simply reply that I just had to have faith and it didn't have to make sense. To me, it was starting to appear like believing in Santa Claus—everybody knew he wasn't real, but pretending to believe made life better, more fun, more beautiful. My friends were also very scared I would end up in hell for even asking such questions. Not being free to question the simplest, most fundamental premises of my childhood faith was the ultimate "because I said so!" The conversation would invariably end with them praying for my eternal soul, all because I questioned the biblical status quo. According to my religious friends, it would seem that God is okay with us humans as long as we don't ask any questions or disagree with what has been written in his book.

Remember the first absolute truths I mentioned at the beginning of this book? Seek and you shall find, knock and the door shall open unto you, and the truth shall set you free. By my friends' reasoning, apparently not. You are free to ask questions, but only as they pertain to a book written almost two thousand years ago. But if you ask the wrong questions, then you go straight to hell. Do not pass Go and do not collect $200. Now that's a God that makes sense! I am being sarcastic here, but please don't get me wrong. I understand completely my friends' point of view. Fear is a very powerful motivator even though that fear may be called faith.

I was soon to make a gradual departure with the organized church. Jesus still had my back, but I have since had to revise my understanding of God altogether. I had to if I was to find happiness and peace. I had to reexamine everything I once believed in. I am eternally glad I did! I know many people have difficulty with the word *God*, and you may be one of them. I completely understand your misgivings as many horrible atrocities have been committed through the ages in the name of God. I feel ya!!! The truth is, I'm not hung up on a word any longer. To quote Shakespeare once again, "A rose by any other name would smell as sweet." It doesn't matter what your name is for this invisible force, it's still a force, a power, and all you have to do to find belief in that force is make an attempt at the assumption that it exists, even if that force is energy itself. It doesn't matter. Then the evidence of your own experience would soon prove sufficient to satisfy your doubts.

I am not by any means asking you to believe something here; I really am not. But I am here to encourage you to ask your own questions, to search for your own truths, to be bold in your adventure. Don't settle for absurd answers. You deserve more than that! This reminds me of another chapter in the story of me. I was thirty-seven years old and waiting for my clothes to dry at our local laundromat in Canon City, Colorado. I was sitting on the concrete wall behind the building, smoking a cigarette. Yes, I use to smoke. As I was sitting and puffing, I began to ponder as I watched the smoke as it left my mouth to dance and twirl on the slight breeze, wandering in and out of the light and shadows cast by the shade of a massive cottonwood tree that overhung the parking lot. I was just sitting there, zoning out, when a question jumped into my head, seemingly from nowhere. I now understand it as now here! I was very present at that moment, a very rare occurrence, especially at the age of thirty-seven.

The question was so profound, it shook the very foundation of all I had learned up to that point. It was to send me on a journey so wonderful, everything before it felt as if I were asleep or dead. This question was to transform me over the decades to come. And nothing since has felt so sweet as those first moments immediately following the receiving of this question.

The question was, "If God made everything, what did he make it out of?" Even at the time of me writing these words, some twenty-five years later, this question still ROCKS my world! I have since posed this question to numerous people, and I have been amazed at the pat answers people came up with. It would seem everybody I would share this question with needed to answer the question immediately, quickly, like handling a hot potato. And instead of letting the question sit just a little bit and gently cool upon their open minds and allow its mystery to reveal its secrets, they had to have an answer NOW. Their egos demanded it.

If you resist the urge to answer quickly, and simply sit and PONDER this question for a bit, it will blow your mind. It's not a question to be answered philosophically. There is no right or wrong answer. You're not going to hell for asking it or answering it, and you have the time you need to consider it. So just ponder the question a bit. What have you got to lose? Ask it in your own voice. Close your eyes, breathe, and I'll repeat the question.

If God made everything, what did he make it out of?

Ponder.

PONDER!

Chapter Seven

Two's Company
Three's ... HOLY COW!

Have you figured out who you are yet? Did you actually PONDER the question in the previous chapter? Or are you just skipping forward hoping I will give you the answer? I will tell you what I have found, but until you do your own pondering, it probably won't resonate with you as much as if you pondered this question for yourself. You might even dismiss it as a novel thought and you will have completely missed a WHOAAAAAA experience, an experience so wonderful, it will overwhelm your senses once you walk into the awareness of the answer and all of its implications. You might also wonder why my question about God has anything to do with who you really are.

Even if you think you may have the answer or are even sure of it, just for the FUN of it, let's revisit that question once more and let's really dissect it this time.

If God made everything, what did he make it out of?

First, I want you to pay extreme attention to the first word, one of the biggest, shortest, and most profound words in our English language. Here, the word *if* does not ask you to believe anything. Rather the word *if* has to be there for us to proceed with the question. Otherwise, no assumption can be made, and the very substance and importance of the question would be lost.

Assume there is a God, a creator, a spark, a big bang—I don't care what you call it. (I can practically hear many of you objecting right now, and you will miss the point of this question if you get hung up on defining God. Believe in your own concept, even if it's energy itself. I'm not going to argue with you, but if you insist on arguing, then argue with yourself. The rest of us will be over here letting this question reveal its answer to us.) Assume this singularity, this condensed thing we call creative intelligence—I'll call it energy for simplicity purposes—this energy existed at the beginning of all time. Here's the important part: NOTHING else existed but this one condensed blob of energy. Try to wrap your brain around this. REALLY try!!! There wasn't SOMETHING called NOTHING; there was only ENERGY, this singular substance, and NO THING outside of itself existed. Not time, not space, not a thing called emptiness, not even a thought. No thing, not even a thing called nothing. There was not some thing and something other than it, there was no thing. Just THING. Energy, only energy. Singular. Are you getting it?

Then suddenly from only ONE source, everything burst forth. (Follow me here.) I used to think in these terms: God took this item from over here and a pinch of that item over there to create this thing and that. But there was NO THING outside of energy. Only energy. Even the big bang theory suggests this. But this question is so simple, it might not compute for most. Most intelligent adult humans I posed this question to came up with all sorts of prerecorded dogma they probably learned as a child but rarely if ever questioned.

Occasionally I would ask a child this question instead of an adult and, because they didn't overthink it, they answered quite simply with the only possible logical answer, void of theology or dogma, superstition or belief. A commonsense, simple, straightforward answer spilled from their innocent lips: "God made everything out of himself."

An Old Testament scripture states "God is love." What if that IS actually what God is? Then Love with a capital L brought forth a million trillion kazillion parts of Love out of LOVE itself. There can be no other answer, for nothing existed outside of LOVE. Love or, rather, God made everything quite literally out of himself.

When I first had this thought, it blew my mind. It also explained so very much. For instance, I had believed since childhood that

God knew everything. How often I was told that God even counted every hair on my head and that is how important I was to him. This all made sense now; God knew everything because he quite literally was and is everything and he loved everything because why wouldn't he? If he were to hate something, since he is in fact, EVERYTHING, then he would in essence be hating himself, which seems impossible or at least very improbable.

Of course, this answer changes everything, unless I am holding onto some notion that there was something else besides the creator in the beginning. That question is truly why the word *if* is such a profound word. Deciding what your choice is to be rests upon the fulcrum of your heart. What do you FEEL is real? "If the creator created everything …???" Did he/it/she really create everything there is? Or did it all just happen? Even if it did just happen, what force put that sequence of happenstance in motion? It's a powerful question this word *if* asks. And IF the creator created everything out of itself, then what does that make me? WHO am I? Who are YOU in the light of this newfound answer? I'll leave you to PONDER this question a bit.

PONDER.

So, now, who are you? I know who you are. Do you? Now we're getting somewhere! There is a great deal involved in this revelation of your true identity. I sincerely hope this BLOWS your mind as it did mine.

I am very happy to finally meet the real you, and, speaking for most of us present, it's about time you showed up. But this newfound revelation raises another question: if I have just found out that I am in fact created by and out of the very substance of God or the creator, then does that mean I am literally ... part of God?

Good question.

Really good question!

I told you it was going to BLOW your mind!

But before we get too lost in this new discovery, let's first review our progress and take stock of what we may have uncovered so far. We have discovered our egos are not our amigos, we've made a peace pact with it, and we have learned of our true identity, our authentic selves, and that now we are connected to everything else in the universe. We—you, me, and God—are quite literally made out of exactly the same thing. LOVE! Like I like to say, "Two's company ... Three's HOLY COW!!!" And now we embark on a grand crusade to find the answer to the second greatest question in the universe:

WHY?

Chapter Eight
Mirror, Mirror

I want you to take a trip with me, but in order to board this train, you'll have to leave all your luggage behind. Luggage is another word for BAGGAGE. You won't be needing it. We are taking this trip in the imagination, and I promise it will be a hell of a ride. I want you to dare to use your imagination, maybe like you never have before. I want you to imagine you are GOD!

No, this is not blasphemy! It is an invitation to explore without limitations the boundless universe as if you were in fact the creator. I am going to guide you on this journey as I have been on these tracks a few times before and have even gotten off a few stops prior to my destination a couple of times. I assure you this trip will be very, very rewarding if you will just sit back and relax, enjoy the scenery and, please, stay on the train, no matter how tempting it may be to disembark early.

I am going to take you on this train far, far back in time. Past the time of the dinosaurs and the cephalopods, before the lava fields dominated the planet. Before our sun flashed its first spark and before the big bang itself. It is the beginning of time and you are God. It is just you and nobody else. There is no sound, no light, no shadow, no touch. No smell and no taste. No sensation whatsoever. There is nothing but your thoughts and that is all. And in your thoughts, there is a knowing, a complete knowing, that you are God and that you are awesome. But "awesome" is only awesome relative to that which is not awesome, so you lack completely the experience of your awesomeness. You only have a concept of awesomeness but no proof. It remains only in your head. But you have no head. You are just a formless blob of love. Pure, condensed love. You know you are awesome, but you have never experienced it. It's like reading a book about swimming— although it is quite enjoyable, it is not the same thing as swimming.

This reminds me of the time I visited Carlsbad Caverns in New Mexico. I had taken my son down into the caverns, guided by a park ranger, and after a mile and a half of glorious stalagmites and stalactites we entered what they call the Big Room, a huge room filled with magnificent columns stretching from the floor to the ceiling of the cave. Scattered among these statuesque columns was every other type of formation you could ever think possible adorning this incredible room. The park ranger told our group of visitors to sit down on wooden benches as he proceeded to educate us on the process and the millennium it took to create these extraordinary structures. He then had us do something that has forever stayed with me; he asked us to hold our hands up directly in front of our faces. The lights in the cave went out.

For a good long minute, my eyes strained hard as they tried to adjust to even the smallest glimmer of light. There was not even the faintest outline of my hand in front of my face. I bumped hard into my nose as I had no sense of space either. I was blind. Had I not been able to feel my face with my hand, it would not have been too difficult to convince me I was asleep. The ranger then had us get as quiet as possible. Not a sound was heard but the occasional someone clearing their throat as if to say, "I'm still here." It was the strangest sensation. Totally dark and almost no sound at all. The slight ringing in my ears seemed to envelop my thoughts, and soon my very thoughts themselves were the loudest things in my head. No matter how hard I tried to hear or see, those experiences were simply not available to me.

A moment of terror washed over me as I imagined myself as a caveman trapped down here a hundred thousand years ago. Following the tracks of a deer that wandered into the cave ever deeper and deeper, I soon lose sight of the tracks and then I lose my way, and just as I am about to give up and turn around, my torch dwindles to a small red ash. I frantically blow on the tiny ember only to watch it soon blow away completely. I am left with silence, blackness, and nothing but the ringing in my ears and the thoughts in my head.

The thought makes me swallow hard.

Now imagine this must have been what it was like for you/ God in the beginning, when it was just you and nobody else and nothing but the powerful thoughts ringing in your consciousness. It must seem strange to BE God but have absolutely no experience as GOD, only a knowing that you are God. Then after a million billion years pass, even the blissfulness of your knowing is no longer good enough for you and a great longing permeates your very being, breaking free from the dark, silent nothingness: a thought, a notion, a PLAN!

"What if I were to create a friend, something else besides me, and we could experience the knowing of each other?" And as that answer fades in the dismal realization that nothing else exists besides myself, it is supplanted by another great and powerful thought: "What if I created beings and a habitat that would all be in ever forgetfulness of its origin? That way, we could have a true and authentic relationship. I shall get to know them and they me. I will give them total free will and the power to create anything they like, with no boundaries whatsoever. I will give them unlimited imaginations, and I will make it fun and intoxicatingly thrilling. This experience I shall call LIFE! And it will forever be the grandest of all experiences and I will BE with them and they with ME and it will be GOOD."

What if? What if that was the way of it?

Of course, you could also ask, "but where did God come from?" and then "where did he, it, they come from?" We could go on forever and ever and never arrive at a final answer. So, at some point, we must decide this is far enough for today. Not because you are not allowed to go further, only that it doesn't profit you to do so.

So, assuming there was only God in the beginning and nothing else, it makes total sense to me that we were the answer to his longing. We are the WHY of his story.

Now, you may not agree with my vision of creation, but I really like my story. It offers an answer I can live with. To me it explains everything about creation and how it all came to be. Now, I don't know the physics of HOW it came to be, but the story works for me better than any other story I've ever heard, and it explains very clearly the second greatest question of all time: WHY?

And as God gazed into the mirror, he saw a beautiful sight; he saw ten trillion billion million creatures staring lovingly back at him.

Chapter Nine
Half Wish ... Full Dish

"Half measures availed us nothing, we stood at the turning point" is a famous line from the book of Alcoholics Anonymous. It speaks to the necessity for a complete immersion or surrender or commitment to undertake whatever task lies before you as you begin your program of recovery. Here in this society it is evident like nowhere else that doing this sobriety thing half-assed is not only foolish, it could very well cost you your life.

If you've ever known or currently know an alcoholic or addict, you can easily understand this all-or-nothing stance. It would seem the entire success of their fellowship depends on nothing less than giving it their all. However, like most humans (I hope I'm not alone), I am usually looking for the easier way. I mean, who wouldn't? Like, can I put in only twenty-five cents and get back a dollar? Please? What if I ask very nicely? What if I whine, yell, or scream? What if I bargain, plead, or beg? What if I sulk, pout, or give you the silent treatment? What if I sue or pass legislation? CAN I PLEASE HAVE A DOLLAR FOR TWENTY-FIVE CENTS? Then there is another kind of human, the resentful type, that insists you pay a dollar for only twenty-five cents' worth, because the last sorry S.O.B. ripped them off.

The old adage "You can't get something for nothing" would, at first glance, appear to be true. I mean, it makes perfect sense, right? That you get back what you put in, yes? REALLY? Are you sure about that? REALLY SURE? Not to take away from your experience, but I've had several great experiences in my life that I had nothing to do with. At least I didn't think so. Looking back through my past, I have taken credit for most of those great things in my life, but if I were to get really honest, I would have to admit I had little to nothing to do with the creation of those events.

I also had experiences that I did not like, and most of those weren't my fault at all. I was quick not to take credit for those negative events. At least that's what I thought for the longest time. I was conveniently taking credit for all the good in my life and almost no credit for the bad. Now, there are those who take credit for all the bad in their lives and never the good, but I don't actually know many of them. I mostly see the first class of people taking credit for the good and not the bad. Sound familiar?

It's as if I was born with a certain level of expectation that everything should work out for me, pretty much just because I'm me. By judging the reactions of people everywhere I look, I think it's safe to assume that just about everybody else feels the same way. It's most evident when I watch people (including myself) not getting their way. And this behavior becomes amplified when they get behind the wheel. Suddenly, many of them become fluent in sign language.

Yes, it would appear that we all have, to some degree or other, a certain entitlement to a good life. Yet there are no guarantees. We weren't born with a contract in hand stating we should get everything we want just because we want it or any real assurances that we should be adorned with all things great simply because we got up this morning. We should go to the front of the line, right? It also became obvious that some do get to the front of the line quite often and others are left outside the doors, begging on the street. But one thing is definitely crystal clear to me and I believe it is something we all have in common: when things don't go our way, we don't much care for it at all.

This assumption that all should be well with us, quite naturally and without effort, seems to be universal to the human condition. So pervasive is this assumption that many devote their entire lives to acquiring all the comforts they can possibly collect. Others, less fortunate, decide to give up their natural desires in exchange for freedom from the burden of want. And I believe many of these people do this simply because the pain of not getting what they truly or maybe even secretly want is simply too great, which reminds me of another story from my childhood.

My six siblings and I were born within an eleven-year period. It was great having a very large family as we always had someone to play with. There were the hours-long games of hide-and-seek in our hundred-year-old barn. There were picnics and birthdays, and my four older sisters taught me more about girls than I could have ever learned from books. By and large, it was an incredibly fun childhood. But there was one rather obvious drawback. There were nine mouths to feed, dress, and everything else involved in living in a large family. We weren't poor but we were definitely not rich, and this became most evident at Christmastime.

Now, my parents did an incredible job with us kids, and I cannot even imagine the pressures my mom and dad must have felt, especially when it came to buying Christmas gifts for seven children. But even so, my parents made Christmas so incredible, these are still some of my favorite memories of all time.

I remember lying on my stomach at the top of the stairs with my closest two sisters and my one brother as we spied silently, trying to stave off sleep long enough to catch a glimpse of Santa Claus as he brought in all of our presents and filled our stockings till they overflowed. We never did catch Santa in the act, but the magic and the anticipation of that night, I can still remember some fifty-plus years later as if it were yesterday. We rested our weary heads upon our crossed arms as we lay on our bellies, gazing at the twinkling lights of the Christmas tree just below, until our eyelids could fight no more and we would fall asleep in a heap at the top of the stairs.

Each one of us children was allowed to pick one item from either the JC Penney catalog or the Sears & Roebuck catalog in the amount of no greater than $10. In the mid-sixties, $10 was about $100 in today's money. I still don't know how my parents did it all. Although $10 was a nice amount, it certainly ruled out many of the really cool gifts in the catalog: the bicycles, the racecar sets, the stereophonic record players, and the chemistry kits. I remember wanting a Charley McCarthy ventriloquist doll more than anything else. If my memory serves, he cost a whopping $50.

Christmas would finally arrive and with great joy, we would open all our gifts, one at a time, and spend the rest of Christmas Day doing nothing but playing, playing, playing, eating fruitcake, and drinking hot chocolate. These are some of the very best memories of my entire life. Life was beautiful that time of year. Christmas was beautiful, MAGICAL!

Then came the first day back at school after Christmas break and my Christmas that had been so huge to me soon dwindled little by little, ever so slightly after each story about the magnificent gifts my friends had gotten for Christmas: stereos, bicycles, go-carts, and racecar sets, even Charley McCarthy dolls. They had all the things I longed for when I perused those catalog pages.

An interesting thing happened to my young mind as it tried to process all the conflicting emotions this stirred within me. My mind had a dilemma. On one hand, I felt I had the best Christmas of all, but, on the other, I did not get what I would have really liked to receive as presents. Even at that very young age, I knew my parents struggled financially to care for us all, and I didn't want to make a fuss, so my innocent heart and mind created something new, a way to have both feelings at the same time.

I carried this coping skill through much of my adult life. I simply decided that I didn't even like those things, so why would I want them? So persuasive was my conviction that I would go out of my way to put down expensive things and activities, stating, "I like the simpler things in life." So began my ego's defensive dislike for anything fancy or expensive, and, most of all, for fun things that cost a lot of money. My ego would rise above my earthly desires, and I would condemn such extravagant activities as below me, even going so far as to call them EVIL.

The truth was, I did want those things—all of those things. But I couldn't admit it because I believed in my heart I would never, ever get them. They were after all, all more than $10. Needless to say, this created a great deal of unhappiness, guilt, and a deep sense of lack in my life. It has taken me a lifetime to undo what was accomplished in just a few impressionable years.

So, do we get something for nothing? From a purely humanistic viewpoint, it may not look like it on the surface. But if I dig a little deeper, I can see many things as an adult that I overlooked as a youth. I can see where I could've clung to gratitude for what was given to me instead of focusing on what was missing: first and foremost, a loving family and a great many playmates. It was an exciting and imaginative childhood, and I wouldn't trade my childhood for anyone else's.

This leads me to the real questions. Did I plan that? Did I earn it? Did I deserve it? And what about the gifts I did receive that Christmas? I may have planned it, because I picked out my $10 gift. I may have even deserved it, because I took the Santa Claus song very seriously: "You better watch out, you better not cry, you better not pout and I'm telling you why." I was a very good boy at Christmastime. But did I earn those gifts? Hardly!

There was only one reason why I received those gifts and all those lovely memories all those years ago—I was loved. I was cherished! The only way I can recognize those incredible gifts is by first cherishing them. To quote Wayne Dyer, "When we change the way we look at things, the things we look at change." I was loved, for sure, no doubt about it. I think about this when I fall into the trap of trying to earn a good life, trying to plan a good life, and then getting resentful if I don't get what I want. The obvious answer is right in front of me, and all I have to do is take my attention off of all the things not going my way for a moment and search for all those things that I have been given for no other reason than that I must be LOVED by something, somewhere.

Changing a lifetime of focusing on what's not happening to focusing on the gifts we have been given is especially difficult to do when one is entrenched in self-pity. But if we can manage to break free from the chains of ingratitude and practice steadily the active focus of appreciation, it can not only make us happier and healthier but it can also, as if by magic, turn the tide of a lifetime of misfortune to fortune. Can you think of anything that you have been given through no effort of your own, or are you drawing a blank?

Let me help you. I would like you to take a pen and paper and start to list all the things you have that you did nothing to earn and have not so much as lifted a finger to create. I'm talking about the small stuff. But the truth is, the REAL TRUTH is, these are the biggest things of all. I'm talking about things like your breath. Many people are, right now, struggling for just one more breath while they lie hooked up to ventilators during this worldwide coronavirus pandemic. Breath, yes, BREATH, the one thing that is absolutely necessary for life itself and for that matter anything else we want as well. It all starts with a BREATH!

"Silly," you might be thinking, but if you take this one thing for granted, guaranteed, you're taking everything else for granted as well. Did you PLAN your breath, EARN your breath, or DESERVE your breath? No! I am suggesting you only have a breath because you are loved, created by and out of love itself. And because you have breath, you have LIFE, the grandest of all adventures, the grandest gesture from a loving universe. Your life force is so strong, even if you hold your breath as long as you can, you will eventually come up for air. You want to live!

There are many, many other things you enjoy that you probably take for granted and had no part in their creation. The really beautiful thing is, if you will actually put pen to paper and list all those things, you can start with a half wish and you will soon find you have a dish so full, it just might overflow. You know what comes next. You guessed it! After you've written a nice long list of all your gifts, I want you to PONDER!

Chapter Ten

Eat Your Veggies

How many times did you hear this as a child: "If you want to grow up big and strong, you have to eat your veggies." Now, just about everybody on the face of the planet knows that vegetables are very, very good for you, jam-packed with vitamins and minerals. However, most children have to be coerced into eating them, or at least reminded. Yes, we humans are funny creatures; the things we typically really want to eat are actually bad for us and the things we don't want to eat are good for us. When we become adults, we are even worse; quite often we have to fight with ourselves to eat what is good for us. The obesity epidemic in the United States is proof of this defiant runaway desire for tasty treats. Back in the 1970s a phrase became very popular and later became a hit song by Larry Groce. I don't think its creator could've realized just how prophetic it was. The newly invented phrase was "junk food junkie." And I am one! Or at least I was.

It wasn't until health issues started to catch up with me that I changed what I ate. I considered it almost a religious rite to eat whatever I wanted, whenever I wanted: two pots of coffee in the morning followed by a full breakfast including waffles and hash browns or maybe even biscuits and gravy, followed by a sandwich and chips or fries for lunch and then a pizza or fried chicken with all the trimmings for dinner. I was drinking a six-pack of Pepsi a day as well. I should have weighed five hundred pounds, but, perhaps thanks to a high metabolism and genetics, I did not.

But I was showing serious signs of hypoglycemia and possibly prediabetes. The effects of so much sugar and carbohydrates in my system left me cranky and lethargic, forcing me to take daily naps in the afternoon. I also suffered from fibromyalgia and had severe GERD. I was forty years old and the wheels were rapidly falling off.

The point of all this dietary confession is not to somehow convince you to eat right; you could not have convinced me then and I'm not going to try and convince you now. It's to illustrate just how defiant I was. It's as if I had a death wish, and maybe that is not far from the truth. I had also felt so physically drained for so long, it had become the norm. When I finally started to figure out what my body needed, I started feeling good again. I cannot imagine going back to my old way of life. But it wasn't easy and it definitely took a long while, a very long while!

I used to think it was a sacrifice to eat good, but the truth is, I was sacrificing feeling good year after year, all for the brief thrill of Milk Duds and popcorn as they melted away over my tongue as I sat in the movie theater or in front of the TV or while I drove in my car. You get the picture. I was a junk food junkie and proud of it. Now, you may be different or have an entirely different reality, but I bet you didn't come by that by accident. No, I bet you were raised with great habits all along. You are one of a lucky few, as the statistics in America show. But this is still not my point.

My point is this: many of us can relate to this food dilemma, but I bet most of us are not just defiant about what we eat. I would guess many of us are also defiant about exercise as well and even more of us are defiant when it comes to spiritual practices. I am this way still. For example, I know how good I feel when I meditate for fifteen minutes a day. It starts my day off much nicer, my life goes smoother, and I am all around a nicer guy when I do this; just ask my wife. But even as good as it apparently makes my life, my mind still tries to figure out the least amount of time I could devote to this practice and still get the maximal benefit. "Maybe I could just meditate in my car on the way to work." Sound familiar?

If you can't relate to any of these scenarios, then you are a superhuman being and I have just one question for you: "Why the hell did you pick up and read this book in the first place?" Go on now, put the book down. There's nothing for you here.

You have already arrived and most of us can't stand you now! Just kidding. But if you can relate, good! That means one thing— you're human. Welcome to the club. Most of us humans have a variety of shortcomings we would love to change, but we just can't seem to find the secret as to HOW to actually make this change happen and, better yet, for it to actually stick.

For example, if you were or are obese, in order to NOT be obese, you would probably and rightfully think or even know that you would have to change your life radically if you would ever wish to be your ideal weight again. That's assuming you once were. Making a radical change would be just what the doctors ordered, right? But here's the rub; knowing what to do rarely will get you very far. Sure, it might be necessary as a starting point, but that is all knowledge of this sort is really good for, to get you started.

Most of us have tried and failed countless times when it came to altering our lives, and never is this more evident than every New Year's. "I'm going to start going to the gym this year." "I'm going to lose fifty pounds." "I'm going to get motivated and change my life." I'm going to meditate." "I'm going to; I'm not going to ..." Blah, blah, blah! And come May 1, when we try on the bathing suit for the first time, we say, "What's the use? Hand me that Butterfinger." We may know what's good for us, but some good that does us.

Don't get me wrong, knowing what to do is important. For instance, year after year people struggling with their weight join spin classes, hot yoga, and gyms, all in the hope of burning off those unwanted pounds. They think this is the answer, but most trainers worth their salt would agree that 80 percent of weight loss is diet and only 20 percent is physical exercise. Yet here we go again, signing up for this or that class, doing the same thing over and over again, expecting different results. This is usually not a case of NOT working hard enough but simply of NOT knowing WHAT is good for you—that is, diet first, exercise second. But even after being informed of what is actually good for us and knowing this truth, few of us make the necessary lasting changes. Why? What could possibly be the problem or, more important, what could be the solution?

It may be simpler than you think. We have all been given FREE CHOICE by a loving creative intelligence of the universe.

It's that simple. And with that incredible freedom of choice, each of us loves to explore the outer boundaries of what that freedom actually means. Many times, we only recognize the right choice by first exploring with great zeal the furthest reaches of the wrong choice, often in the unconscious hope of finally arriving at the place where we are right now. We have run out of ideas. Our own thinking and willpower have failed us. This is an AWESOME place, a PERFECT place, a very SPIRITUAL place! A place of SURRENDER! For it's only when we're out of ideas that we find ourselves open to suggestions from the mysterious power that creates worlds. Madness, you might say. We choose wrong so we can find what's right?

What else could explain why so many otherwise sane people intentionally set out on a path of the deliberate destruction of their bodies? It defies nature. It defies logic, at least conventional logic. But I believe our paths are more about exploration than they are about anything else. Let's say, then, for the sake of argument that you've explored all you *want* of what you DON'T *want* and have now arrived at a place where you have decided you *want* something different for yourself, something better, the right choice. You may ask: What then? What is missing, what is the magic ingredient, and why should I believe you when I've tried and failed so many times before? Is there a secret to success?

YES, I believe I may be able to help. Remember the title of this book, *You Selfish Bastard*. You must be selfish enough to care about yourself and do something about it. The following outline is exactly the process I had to follow if I was to ever free myself from any all-consuming and most disagreeable shortfalls. I was going to have to, first, identify the problem; second, to decide to do something about it; third, to not go it alone; and, fourth, to utilize that loving universe I mentioned earlier if I was to ever hope to be free. I was going to need some big MOJO, MAGIC, POWER outside of my scope of reference. I was going to need the power of the universe, the power that creates worlds.

Call this power anything you like, but it became evident to me that my own power was simply not adequate for the task at hand. For if it had been, I would've already arrived at my desired destination. Lord knows, I've tried hard enough.

Yes, power is what is called for whenever we want to change or rebuild our life. I mean that metaphorically and quite literally.

If you want to build your life into something different, you are going to need power and a lot of it. Vegetables provide power, ice cream not so much. Get my drift? You don't have to feel like eating your vegetables in order to eat your veggies. You don't have to enjoy the taste in order to enjoy the benefits of eating what's good for you. And you don't have to feel like doing spiritual work in order to take the action and reap the rewards. This might be a good place to interject one of my favorite phrases, "fake it till you make it." You can fake enjoying your veggies, and guess what? After a while, you will actually begin to enjoy eating them. But even if you never develop a taste for veggies (which will not happen), you will, nevertheless, enjoy the benefits of digesting this power-packed food group immediately. Get the metaphor?

Whenever we set out to change our lives, there is a point we all get to, where we must get to, and that is that it's natural for it not to feel natural. New behavior never feels natural. What feels natural is eating a pint of Ben & Jerry's at midnight, right? This is where you will need to use your new power and a good dose of willpower as well, and FAKE IT TILL YOU MAKE IT! So, shush up, stop your complaining, sit up straight, and eat your VEGGIES!... Spiritually speaking.

Chapter Eleven
A Powerful Story

In what seems a lifetime ago, I was a heating and air-conditioning repairman. I was eighteen years old. I am so glad for that training because within the two or three years that followed, I learned how to use my hands, not only for heating and air conditioning but also for plumbing, electrical work, and carpentry. I had learned to be a jack-of-all-trades. I learned so well that this knowledge came in handy some twenty years later (2001) when my second wife and I, with the help of our four boys, built our own home from the ground up. We did everything—plumbing, electrical work, and construction. It was something I had wanted to do all my life.

Throughout my few short years as a repairman, I was on lots of different jobsites, everything from a remodel to completely new homes. Each of those jobs started with a plan, a blueprint. There was also the list of lumber, fixtures, wiring, etc. If it was a remodel, we figured out what was staying and what was being torn out. When it was a new homesite, the ground was prepared first and a nice solid foundation set. What we needed depended on if we were completely starting over or just making improvements.

Once the building had begun, we needed lots of tools to finish the job. This was where the work really began. We might have been able to finish our house using hand tools only, but it would've been very hard work and taken a very long time. Luckily, we did not have to do that excruciating labor because we had electricity at the jobsite: POWER! Because we used POWER tools, the job went a lot smoother, quicker, and easier, and it came out better. But there was a simple catch—power tools would not have done us much good if we never plugged them in. Power tools run on power.

After you plug power tools in, it takes a little skill to use them, and there's only one way to gain these skills: practice! And the only way to practice is by doing. Talking about building a new home is not at all the same as building a new home. This is the difference between talking the talk and walking the walk. Get the metaphor?

Now that we've started work, it is apparent we have to not only pick the right tool for the right job. We also have to understand what the tool does and to use that tool for that purpose only. In other words, you may use a nail gun to drive a nail, but it makes a terrible circular saw. More explicitly (spiritually speaking), the tool of honesty is a great power tool when used upon yourself, but it quite often mutilates or even destroys completely when used on others. It then becomes brutal honesty. The tool of open-mindedness works great on yourself but loses all benefit and causes a great rift when forged as a weapon against others. Likewise, the tool of willingness works wonders upon yourself but is totally useless when you apply it to others. We cannot will anyone else to do anything. Get the picture yet? Tools are only to be used on yourself! When used on others, they become weapons, weapons of mass destruction, weapons of war.

But wait! There's more. Perhaps most important of all, you will need to always remember to plug your tools into power. Sound elementary? You'd be surprised how many of us try to use power tools without power. You might be wondering, "how do I find the power?" You have to search for it! I remember many times arriving at the jobsite and having to plug into several different extension cords before I found one with "the juice." Remember "seek and you will find?" You will absolutely find what you are searching for, but there is also the flipside; the best way to never find the necessary power to change your life is not to look for it. So, if you really want change, grab your tools, plug them in, and get busy.

Chapter Twelve

Come What May

"Que Sera, Sera," a song written by Jay Livingston and Ray Evans, was made popular in 1956 by Doris Day in the Alfred Hitchcock movie *The Man Who Knew Too Much*. It soared to popularity in the years just prior to my birth. The chorus goes, "Que sera, sera, whatever will be will be. The future's not ours to see, que sera, sera." I grew up singing that song, and it is one of those melodies that just sticks in your head. I know it did mine, and oftentimes I would find myself humming or singing it, whether I wanted to or not, all day long. Great tune!

What does this mean, "que sera, sera?" It's a mixture really, a blend between Spanish and Italian through a little movie magic. It translates loosely to "what will be will be." As with most songs that gain popularity, I wonder sometimes if it's just another nice, pleasant song, or does it ring of something profound in the human experience? Why did it gain such fame, and could it have become so popular if it didn't resonate with people everywhere on some level? When songs through the ages have gained such a profound foothold in our societies, perhaps they hold some hidden secrets about our existence here on earth. I also wonder if these songs might be, in fact, hidden messages from other realms and are spiritual in nature, containing otherworldly, meaningful messages from beyond.

This may seem a little nuts, but, believe it or not, many people, myself included, have made the erroneous assumption that only people who are on a decidedly spiritual path can relate to spiritual implications, and unless the particular piece of music in question is presented as a spiritual message from the onset, then it would automatically fall into the category of "secular" music with a secular message, holding nothing of spiritual value for the listener. This assumption may be very far from the truth and if we persist in this assumption, then we are well on our way to spiritual segregation, missing much of what this world has to offer simply because it does not bear the stamp of obvious spiritualism.

Well, I've got news for you, my friend: we are ALL on a spiritual quest. It's just that some of us are unaware of it. But even so, when something comes along that rings of spiritual truth, it's as if our souls come alive at the ringing of it, like a huge chapel bell or an ancient Chinese gong. Many times these bells wake us from our spiritual slumber. "Que Sera, Sera" is one of those bells. It rings of freedom and a complete willingness to let things go. The melody reflects such a lighthearted attitude, it is almost irresistible to the passing ear. There have been numerous songs over the years that we find ourselves humming or singing, and the true gift of many of these melodies is that they make us feel alive. They evoke—wait for it—happiness, right? It is my profound belief that if something truly makes you happy, it can't be bad, *truly* being the optimal word here.

But this chapter isn't about the popularity of the song "Que Sera, Sera." It's about the message it contains or, rather, implies. The words of this song may suggest an almost apathetic stance and a resignation to fate. "Whatever will be will be" certainly points in that direction. However, if we listen to the words of the song as it dances harmoniously with the melody, we will soon be caught up in a feeling of carefreeness, lightheartedness, and happiness. I believe this was the intent of the song's writers. I believe this was their real gift to us, a divine gift.

But that is still not the entire point of this chapter either, at least not completely. But it does POINT to the POINT, if you catch my drift. The song, words, and melody all sweep us along on a feeling of happiness and freedom, of carefreeness, of surrender, of letting go. And nearly all of us extract the exact same feeling from this song. It would appear to be universally understood. And what a great word *carefree* is. Nearly everybody knows and understands this word and, better yet, desires it, desires to be it!

To be carefree appears to be the absolute pinnacle of the human experience. What could be greater than that unbelievably high feeling of being carefree? Everybody knows what carefree feels like, and I bet most know the true meaning. Here's what the word means, according to the dictionary.

carefree
<u>**adjective**</u>
care·free | \ 'ker-ˌfrē \
Definition of *carefree*
: free from care: such as
a: having no worries or troubles spent a *carefree* day at the lake
b: To be free from responsibility

"To be free from worry or troubles," the dictionary states, but it also states, "to be free from responsibility." This latter description is usually the one that has most of us close the book forever on actually obtaining a truly carefree life. After all, if we are indeed free from care and responsibility, then we wouldn't care about our responsibilities, and wouldn't it then be safe to assume this act of carefreeness would make us out to be very, very SELFISH?

Can you be carefree and have a job? Can you be carefree and have a wife, a husband, kids? Can you be carefree if you're a minister, a doctor, a lawyer, a prince, a candlestick maker? Can you, for that matter, have responsibility and still feel carefree, or is one interdependent on the other? Is being carefree even possible as an adult? What a dilemma! Everybody loves to feel carefree and yet, as adults, we intentionally burden ourselves with the cares of the world. What gives?

It would seem as we grow into young adults we are judged by our ability to shoulder responsibility. Yet as children we had been granted a vision of heaven, a delightful place of joyful expression and play. But when we grow up we are not permitted entrance ever again. The Amusement Park of Life has been closed to us. We have exceeded the height requirement to ride any of its fanciful rides. And if we did somehow figure out how to steal our way back into the amusement park, our gangly height would soon give us away as adults and we would forever be branded as self-serving, childish, and selfish individuals caring only about ourselves. This we must not have. We want to play but we are forbidden. So we suffer in silence as we mope, head down, slowly, sluggishly away from the joyful sounds of the amusement park. And as we somberly walk along, every so often we break our self-imposed silence by humming a soft and quiet melody, "Que Sera, Sera." We smile ever so briefly.

Chapter Thirteen
CRAP

CRAP! CRAP! ALL CRAP! That's right, the end of the last chapter is all CRAP! And yet so many of us subscribe to, endorse, propagate, and actually LIVE that CRAP! What crap? This crap about growing up and no longer being able to live carefree. It's crap! CRAP! CRAP! CRAP! CRAP!!

All my life I've had teachers, adults, siblings, parents, and supposedly well-intentioned fellow human beings tell me, "Oh, grow up!" or "You're such a big kid!" or "a boy and his toys," they say in an especially condescending tone. It wasn't until I was fifty years old that I finally answered one such lady when she mockingly stated, "D. Arthur, you're such a big kid." She did not mean it as a compliment, but I answered with a joyful and hearty laugh and stated quite confidently, "Why, that's the nicest thing anyone has ever said to me. Thank you!" Her jaw dropped as I turned and walked away. No one has said those words to me since, not because I have since grown up, but because I no longer disapprove of my own childlike demeanor. In fact, I celebrate it.

I feel sorry for those who would try to control the joyful outburst of themselves and others and now realize, quite compassionately I might add, that these serious folk, prone to control, are actually jealous and would give anything to cast away their choking shackles of self-imposed judgment and fear. Actually, it's just FEAR, as judgment is merely fear's bastard child, born of the unholy wedlock of fear and self-loathing. Yes, self-hatred and fear got together and produced their hideously ugly child and named her Judgment. Judy for short.

Please don't get offended if you know a Judy, or if your name is Judy, or if you're actually Judge Judy. I simply meant that it is out of self-hatred and fear that our judgment is born. Here, our old nemesis, the ego, may pipe in to defend. "I don't hate myself," it may shout in disapproval. But I must tell you judgment is certainly not born out of love for oneself. No, this unwanted offspring that would rob us of our joy speaks ever so eloquently in defense of our necessity to take things seriously. And we do this, all because we simply don't know any better. We don't know we have another choice besides giving up our carefreeness in exchange for what we think is our responsibilities. We label it any number of seemingly grown-up titles: facing reality, getting real, taking it seriously, paying the piper and, my personal favorite, you've made your bed, now you must lie in it. All the while we also agree that a carefree life is an admirable goal. Just how do we approach living a childlike and carefree life when we can barely hear over the booming voice of reason screaming in our ears?

First and most important, we must decide that we *deserve a carefree life* and that nothing else could be of greater value than for us to live *joyfully*, *happily*, and *carefree*. Without this decision, we simply will not have the necessary direction we need. It would be like embarking on a great voyage on an endless sea without a heading. So we must set our course. A carefree life, here we come!

At this time, I would like to introduce a word that is common in spiritual practices but not very common anywhere else. The word is *paradox*, and here's what Webster has to say about it.

paradox
<u>noun</u>
par·a·dox | \ 'per-ə-ˌdäks , 'pa-rə- \
Definition of *paradox*
1: a <u>tenet</u> contrary to received opinion
2a: a statement that is seemingly <u>contradictory</u> or opposed to <u>common sense</u> and yet is perhaps true
b: a self-contradictory statement that at first seems true
c: an argument that apparently derives self-

contradictory conclusions by valid deduction from
acceptable premises

So here's the paradox: to seek a carefree life may at first
glance appear to be a noble cause, but, upon closer examination,
this quest also falls under the very description of SELFISHNESS.
Pursuing your own happiness or pleasure, considering your own
needs, being concerned with your own happiness, that's selfish,
right? And by definition, seeking to be carefree then would be an
entirely selfish act.

This is quite a paradox. On one hand, focusing on your own
happiness appears to be selfish and, on the other, it is obvious
that a carefree life is synonymous with a happy life and desired
by almost everybody. So, which is it? Selfish or not? It's BOTH!
That is why it's a paradox. And it does raise the question as to
whether selfishness is always a bad thing.

I think to better understand this paradox we may want to go
back to the previous chapter about understanding the very nature
of life itself, of creation, and of our creator. We have to go back to
LOVE. Life is love! Love is life!

If LOVE created everything out of LOVE ENERGY itself,
and if I've chosen to believe that God is actually made out of
LOVE, then love is what God does and is. If love created life,
then life is also love. It stands to reason I must also be loved by
God, by LOVE. I am, after all, alive. I have life. There is no other
obvious choice. And why would God not love me? He created me
from love itself. It also stands to reason, then, that to hate or not
love oneself would in fact be committing a very ungodly act.

Please stop and ponder that sentence for a moment. To not
love oneself or even to hate oneself is to hate that which created
you. If you indeed know WHO you are and what you're made of,
then, once more, LOVE is the only proper response to yourself.
Loving yourself **IS** God's will for you. You were created to be
loved.

You might ask: Can't we just focus on others? Forget about
ourselves? Think about them and their needs and put away this
selfish discussion altogether? Why must we now be talking about
loving ourselves? Do we have to go there? Yes, we must go there
because you can't have one without the other. You can't have a
giver without a receiver, a lover without the loved. You can't have

a teacher without a student, a doctor without a patient, or a solution without a problem. And to want or even expect to always be the giver and never the receiver is to deny yourself the incredible humility required to accept help and LOVE from others. Whether it be help received by money, compliments, or gifts, it doesn't matter. And humility, as we all know, is the opposite of egotism. To be humble enough to graciously accept love, even from ourselves, would then also appear to be the opposite of egotism and consequently the opposite of selfish, right?

Also, if we are always the giver and refuse to be the recipient, we are in essence expecting others to do that which we ourselves are unwilling to do, rendering us hypocrites and, you guessed it, very, very selfish. So, if you want to be less selfish, grant others the joy of loving you. Grant yourself the joy of loving yourself. Allowing others the thrill of giving is a gift we can offer freely, knowing now that the circle is complete.

The divine paradox is that to love others is in fact the same as to love ourselves. To love ourselves is to love others. And because we are all made of the same stuff (LOVE), when we love others, when we love ourselves, we are loving GOD. We are ONE. Once you have decided you are worthy of love, being carefree is not only desirable but also your birthright. And not only is it your desired state, your birthright, but dare I say it is your holy and divine responsibility. What a paradox!!!

What does loving yourself have to do with living a carefree life? EVERYTHING! You must first recognize your true value to God, to us, and to yourself in order to understand just how important it is to live life carefree and to be selfish enough to believe you're worth it. YOU HAVE TO CARE ENOUGH TO BE CAREFREE! For in having learned to love yourself, you know the importance of freeing yourself of burdens, and, from this light and carefree existence, you now have something of great value to GIVE.

Chapter Fourteen
It's about Time

A long, long time ago, in a galaxy far, far away ...

Time! The final frontier. The only frontier ...

These are the voyages of YOU! To boldly go where few men and women have gone before, to seek out a LIFE and all its hidden GLORIES. To explore brave new worlds and new adventures. To SEEK and to FIND! I hope you can forgive me for being so bold as to quote some very famous space odysseys. But what better way to illustrate this chapter?

Since the advent of science fiction, many TV shows and movies have taken us on incredible adventures; exploring the *Outer Limits* of our space/time continuum. There's a little *Back to the Future* in that one. But, seriously, since so many of us have watched these awesome shows and films, we have a new sense about what this thing called time actually is. Many of us know it from a purely intellectual foundation, but just how many of us spend much time in it? In time? Consciously aware of time? Here, we must take a *Quantum Leap* forward to a place rarely visited by humankind, the ever-present but very illusive moment, NOW! What is NOW? Why is it so important?

First of all, time is all we ever really have. It's true, I promise, but just because it's the only thing we really have, it is no small matter. We even use words regularly without noticing their implied importance, words like *lifetime* or the phrase "it was the time of our lives." Many of us go through life constantly on our way to some far-off destination, some distant future event that will somehow enable us to suddenly enjoy the time we have. *When I get married, when I retire, when I have enough money, when I get a girlfriend, when I go on vacation, when I get a divorce, then, I'll be happy.* We put off our happiness until "someday." And all the while the clock keeps on ticking. Some of us lose years, some lose decades, and some even go their entire lives without really showing up for a single minute of it. We chase the carrot on the end of the string, all the while promising ourselves we will stop soon, we will take a break soon, we will "enjoy" soon. Enjoy what? When?

Time, yes, time, the precious gift given to all of us. Every single person on the face of planet earth has been granted time. And thus time, it would seem, is inherently related to life. You can't have one without the other; without life, nothing could witness the passing of time. Without time, life is nonexistent. We must be born, live, and die, all within the impersonal embrace of time. Our lifetime.

We all know of time because we experience its passing; there was yesterday, today, and tomorrow. The before, during, and after. The beginning, the middle, and the end. Yes, we are aware of time and even of concepts like the beginning of time and the end of times. Time fascinates us, at least enough that we talk about it once in a while, watch a movie or TV show about it, but do we really examine it? Really understand it? Really LIVE in it? Many of us would rather think about past times or the future and miss completely this enormous gift laid in our very laps. Present time. More precisely, NOW!

There it is again. How trite. Most of us have heard the expression "now is the only time," but have you ever really thought about just what that saying could actually mean to us? NOW is the only time. I hope we can all come to the obvious conclusion that now actually IS the only time, that there is no other time than NOW, this present moment. Past and future do not actually exist. Can you wrap your mind around that one? We all have a past, right? But do we really? Or are we perpetually in the moment with only the illusory concepts of past and future? We can't access the past (live in the past); we can only remember it in our mind. Likewise, we can only experience the future through our imaginations, our minds. Either way, both past and future are all in our heads, right? Let me present for your consideration and pondering this question: "How long is NOW?"

No! Really! Try to answer this question. "How long is now?" I've asked many people this very same question and got back almost identical responses whether from a young adult, a rabbi or minister, or just some hippy dude down at the beach. Here's what they all answered. "It's a blink of an eye. It's a fraction of a second. It's a millisecond. It's here and then it's gone before you know it."

I would then inquire, "So a millisecond is the shortest moment of NOW?" They would stop to think a moment. "What if I were to cut that millisecond in half? Then cut it half again and half again? Could I ever get to an absolute zero of measurement of time?"

They would look at me, puzzled, and answer, "No, it would obviously go on indefinitely."

I would ask, "Forever?" They would nod in agreement.

I would then ask, "But does NOW ever expire? I mean, by the time you notice it, it is gone, right? Does that mean it is not NOW, now?"

"Of course, it is NOW, now," they would always state. Even the hippie agreed with that one. "It's always NOW," they would retort.

"But how long is it NOW?" I would press. "A minute, a month, a year? How long does NOW go on?"

"Forever." They would almost always arrive at this most amazing conclusion. It doesn't matter how you try to shorten time or extend it; the answer is the same on both ends—eternity. Or like I like to say, forever and ever, hallelujah, hallelujah!

Eternity!

What a concept. Having no beginning and no end. Think about that for a moment. Really ponder it. I pondered this for some time, and it became obvious to me that TIME is what we've been searching for all along and that eternity could possibly be the eternal now, yes? This eternal moment, this NOW, this ever-present present has always been with us and forever shall be. Which leads me to an important question. "If NOW is the only TIME, where would God live? When would God live?"

It would be safe to say that many religions refer to God as the Alpha and Omega, the beginning and the end, and that God has been associated with the concept of eternity since the beginning of the notion of eternity. Since most believers agree that God is eternal, it's not a far stretch to think that God lives forever and is forever, right? Follow me here closely. So, if God lives in eternity, forever and ever, and now cannot be measured either by shortness or by length and is eternal and forever and ever, wouldn't it make sense that NOW is actually where GOD exists? When God exists? And if that is where God lives, then might that place, that TIME, also be referred to as the Kingdom of Heaven, if you will?

Now, keep following because this may make a lot of sense to us and would imply that if we wanted to connect with God, we could only do so in the here and now. It also becomes obvious that God would not be able to connect with us when we're in fear because fear is a projection into the nonexistent future. It would also mean that God could not be felt when I am full of guilt, shame, or remorse as those all exist in the equally nonexistent past. So too are revenge, grudges, or hurt feelings—all past. If NOW is the only real domicile of God the creator, then if we want to make contact, we must do it NOW, in the present. We must reach out here, right where we are, not where we would like to be or from a place of deserved or undeserved holiness or sinfulness (past deeds), but here, just as I am, right now, warts and all.

I'm not saying God cannot hear us as we cry and wail. I'm not saying God the creator doesn't feel our pain and anguish and hear our prayers. I'm saying we cannot connect to the power of the creator, the peace of his presence, the unbelievable calm that we can experience, until we finally surrender our past and our future. Only then can we enter into communion with the creator of the universe. Only then do we find solace, peace, relief NOW.

There's so much more to this creator/God/love/time thing than I can possibly put into one chapter, but I will say this. Time, this precious moment right here and now, is the greatest of all gifts we have ever received or ever shall receive forevermore. Within this moment lies the keys to the kingdom and love eternal. It is this very moment when we can always meet our maker. For all of us shall, one day or another. By the way, do you know the greatest gift you can give to another? Your time.

Chapter Fifteen

HOOVER

This SUCKS! This analogy actually sucks. Literally! For this is a story about vacuum cleaners. Actually, it is a story about us. All of us. About life. About ourselves and about our relationships. This is a metaphor, a parable, a story, a truth ...

Imagine that when all of us are born, we are each given a small patch of carpet on which to live out our days, about six feet by six feet square. Some carpets are shag, some are Berber, some are indoor/outdoor, but all of us are given a very comfortable carpet on which to live OUR LIFE. Mine is a deep forest green, short-pile rug. Anyway, we are all given this carpet and it is here and only here where we can live.

Now, we can travel, of course, go places and do a wide variety of things during our lives but, we all must do them from our private carpet. It's our magic carpet ride. Which brings me to my story within this story. A lifetime ago, I was going along, minding my own business ... I must stop myself there as that is not entirely true. Actually, I was minding everybody else's business. If I had been minding my own business, my life, the carpet of my life, would not have become so totally filthy, cluttered, and stinky. The deep forest green color had become barely visible under the layers and layers of dirt. Year after year, the unnoticed dust had accumulated all about me. I was a mess. My six-feet-by-six-feet life was a disaster. I didn't know what to do and I didn't know how my carpet, my life, had gotten so far out of control.

This may seem a lighthearted metaphor, but I assure you it's not. My life had turned unbelievably dark. The black grime of guilt had stained my soul/my carpet so deeply, I was sure it could never again be that beautiful deep forest green rug I had once enjoyed. Until one day, some wonderful friends flew up on their magic carpets and I noticed just how beautiful and tidy their carpets all were. Their colors were so bright. I was immediately embarrassed of the mess I had been flying around in. But they were very kind and made me feel quite welcome. They never pointed out the disaster of my carpet nor did they call attention to the cleanliness of theirs. They just rode alongside me as we flew over mountains and meadow alike.

Then the day came, one magical day, when I asked them, "How do you have such nice, beautiful carpets to ride around on?" They all smiled and laughed hard. At first I thought they were laughing at me, but then the one riding the brightest of the carpets—it was a sunburst orange tweed—zoomed up alongside me and said, "My carpet didn't always look this good. Why, my carpet made yours look like it had just been through a car wash."

I looked at him in disbelief. He added, "In fact, mine was piled so high and full of crap, it measured six feet by six feet by six feet. They call me the Cube: that's how dirty my carpet was."

I was shocked, as there wasn't even a speck of dirt visible upon that sultry orange rug, not one thing out of place. Puzzled, I asked, "HOW?"

The man with the burnt-orange-colored carpet lowered his head and looked up at me through the tops of his eyes barely visible from under the fertile growth of eyebrow hair and said, "It's simple, really. All that junk cluttering your carpet, get rid of it, throw it over the side, and find your Hoover."

"My Hoover?"

"Your Hoover," he stated again. "Everybody's got a Hoover. You've got one. I've got one. We've all got a Hoover, you know, a vacuum."

"You lost me. What do you mean we all have a Hoover?" I asked a bit cautiously.

"We all have a Hoover, a vacuum to clean up our messes. We were born with it."

"I don't think I have a Hoover," I replied.

"You can't find it because it's buried under all that garbage you carry around. It took me months to find my Hoover. Now, you wouldn't think you could lose a vacuum cleaner on a six-feet-by-six-feet rug, but you can and it happens all the time. Usually we get so busy looking at other people's crap, and maybe even trying to find their vacuum cleaners for them, that we forget about our own vacuums. That's how I lost my vacuum: too busy looking at everybody else's crap. I suspect that's why you can't find yours."

"I guess you might be right," I muttered.

"You see, people would much rather focus on other people's dirt than on their own. It's just what we do. I can see your junk super easy, but when it comes to mine, I can't even find my own vacuum cleaner! You get my drift?" He rolled his eyes and let go a belly laugh that shook me to my core. I knew he was telling me the truth.

"There are even those who think they can actually clean someone else's carpet for them. They think they are being helpful, but they're not. All they seem to do is make a bunch of fake vacuum sounds as they just move shit around. Varoooooom, varoooooom, varoooooom, pushing crap everywhere and usually leaving a bigger mess than when they started. Thanks a bunch, guys, thanks a bunch, right? Worthless, absolutely worthless."

"Why would that be worthless? Aren't they just trying to help? You can't think it's bad to want to help people," I said in defense of all things good and virtuous.

"Oh, no, they're making a mess of things all right, because they simply don't know. They haven't stopped long enough to find out."

"Find out what?"

"They haven't figured out how to use their own vacuum; they haven't even unpacked the damn thing. It says right in the instructions—why doesn't anyone ever read the instructions?" he stammered off into a soft mumble. "If they would just take the time to unpack their vacuum and open their eyes and read the instructions, they would save themselves, they would save all of us, so much trouble. The instructions explain everything about your Hoover: how to clean it, how to take care of it, and how to use it. You see, that's the thing that fraps my gizzard more than anything. They don't even know how to use the gawl-darn thing!"

"So how DO you use it? Isn't it obvious?"

"You would think so, wouldn't you? The instructions are

simple. 1. Unpack your Hoover. 2. Install the hypoallergenic filter, securing the bag over the nozzle with an elastic band. 3. Unwrap the power cord. And this is where most people set the instructions down because they are sure they got this. Worthless! They forget to read the most important thing of all!"

"What's that?"

"YOU GOT TO PLUG IT IN! It doesn't do a damn thing if you have no power. You got to plug it in. You might think I'm being silly, but it's true! I forget to plug mine in all the time and sometimes I think I'm plugged in, but then I end up—after making another mess—finding out that the cord slipped out of the socket again. So I gotta keep checking to make sure I'm plugged in. Otherwise, I'll never get any work done. Worthless! Just worthless!" He laughed mockingly at himself. "Oh, and there's one more thing."

"There's more?"

"Really important!"

"Okay."

"Your Hoover, my Hoover, everybody's Hoover, comes with only a three-foot-long cord. Just long enough to perfectly clean your own carpet. Try to use your Hoover on someone else's carpet and it comes unplugged every time. You have no power to clean other people's magic carpets."

"But, do you mean we can never really help anybody else? We can't help them clean? We can only help ourselves? That doesn't seem very nice; it seems selfish, even! I thought we were supposed to help those who cannot help themselves."

After a long pause of silence, he took a deep breath and, staring at me, eye to eye, unblinking, he stated with unwavering clarity, "Of course you can help people, but you first must decide if they really want help. You see, there are four types of people in this world. First, there are those who don't care about how messy their carpets are and, in fact, sometimes they are very proud of all their dirt, going so far as to give pet names to their favorite junk. You try and remove any of these treasured artifacts of dysfunction and you are sure to get blasted. You can't help these people at all, no matter how disturbing their messes are to you.

"Then there are the types of people who beg for help but secretly don't want to give up a single thing. They want to have their cake and eat it too. Sure, they say they want a clean carpet and even solicit your help, but they are quite willing to let you do most of the work. When you are not looking, they attach rubber bands to each of their favored items, so as you hurl one item over the side, it appears to be gone, but as soon as the rubber band stretches as far as it can, gravity gives way to tension and finally bungees it back. Just as you're busy on one side of their magic carpet, tossing yet another item over the side, the earlier chucked items are popping right back into place. This is very exhausting work and quite often you find yourself asking, 'Didn't we just get rid of this shit?'

"You can actually help some of these people sometimes, but only when they get good and tired of their mess and if you refuse to do their work for them. Your best shot is to inspire them with your life and how free of clutter your carpet is, offering help only as far as they are willing to let their trash go. You cannot desire something for someone else, but you can inspire them. You can inspire a desire.

"The third class of people are perhaps the saddest as they are so scared of clutter and junk collecting on their carpets, they simply don't go anywhere, do anything, or take any chances. They leave their magic carpets in the garage. What a pity. They have learned the best way to keep their carpet clean is to make no mistakes. They are the ones following all the rules. But life is messy, it's supposed to be, and that is why we all have vacuum cleaners. These people think they are keeping their carpets spotless, but their inactivity has attracted a thick layer of dust over time. These unfortunate souls have a very difficult time seeing their mess and are quite sure they have none. But their carpets have grayed by the passage of time to such degree their color is no longer visible. Their magic carpets may have never turned into complete disasters, but they haven't really explored life beyond the safety of their garage either. They might secretly wish for a little filth but are too terrified of its consequences.

"These people are much like the first; you cannot help them for they are quite sure they don't need help. They must first get good and tired of their current surroundings and desire something different. When this happens, quite often something drastic occurs to prompt them to leave the garage and risk the great outdoors, to risk life. And at other moments, they can be inspired by your joy, your freedom, and your amazing Hoover.

"And finally there are those like yourself who have made a real mess of things. These delightful fortunate souls have really lived and are now desiring something different. They are not only inspired by the hope of freedom and joy but also propelled forward by the previous pain of the years of attracting crap. These are the folks you can most help because they will ask you, in so many words, 'How did you get such a nice carpet?' Then you can show them how to find their own Hoover too."

Chapter Sixteen
But Crack

As you may have guessed by now, I went through a life-changing experience when everything I had come to believe in was shaken to its core. Like an 8.0 on the Richter scale, my life was demolished. Without going into the specifics of my demise, the REAL interesting story is in the process I went through of rebuilding my life.

After my structure (life) came tumbling down all about me and I was left sifting through the rubble in the hopes of finding something of value, I cleared away enough debris to catch a glimpse of my foundation, the base upon which I had built my life. The structure was severely damaged and as I cleared away even more, I could see the full extent of this serious foundational flaw. I could, for the first time, really examine the bedrock upon which my life, a towering but shaky domicile, was built.

What I found as I poured over, with desperate eyes, my old concrete foundation inch by inch was that at the center lay a huge and very deep crevasse. The floor had turned and buckled when the great upheaval hit me and shook my house into this unusable scrap pile. This crevasse, this crack, had a name. It was BUT. This was my BUT crack.

"But crack?" you may ask. Yes, my BUT crack.

My foundation was beyond repair. No matter what I tried, I just couldn't rid myself of my But crack... Not as long as the old foundation was in place. It became obvious I would have to tear up the old footing and replace it with a smooth, solid, and reinforced concrete slab that would withstand the turmoil and trials of life. As I stood over the immense crack that had destroyed my life, I realized a fundamental flaw in my thinking, and it went all the way back through my childhood. I realized also that I may have had help in the pouring of my old, inferior foundation.

You see, I had always believed God loved me and he loved you too, but over time and with a lot of different influences, including erroneous religious studies and listening to many guilt-ridden sermons, each of these corrosive elements began to overwhelm my belief structure. Little by little, "buts" were introduced into my otherwise innocent philosophy. These seemingly well-intentioned little "buts" started building upon each other and, like a little creek forging into ever larger and larger rivers, the final result was the great chasm over which I now stood. My grand "but" crack.

It started innocently enough: God loves you, "but" you can't lie. God loves you, "but" you can't cuss, "but" you must wear a tie, "but" you must take off your hat, "but" you must cut your hair, "but" you must dress up, dress down, pray this way, pray that way, be baptized this way or that. "But" you mustn't drink, dance, or enjoy sex. The "buts" just seemed to go on and on. All the while, the little drop that was my truth, "God loves you," was lost in the torrent that raged through my understanding, eroding the very fabric of my soul.

And as I stood at the edge of this great abyss, I knew what I must do. I was to rebuild my life upon one truth and one truth only. My foundation was to be as smooth as glass, as strong as a diamond, and as unshakable as the heavens. My foundation upon which I was to build everything to come was simply, "God loves me …"

PERIOD!

And he loves you too …

PERIOD!

When I have held to this simple truth, everything else falls gently into place. I have endured many storms and tempests since that fateful day more than two decades ago, and since I have re-poured my foundation, I am happy to report, it is still holding strong. The mansion I have since built upon it has provided warmth, shelter, and comfort to all who enter.

Chapter Seventeen
Victim vs. Villain

This chapter is dedicated to the villains and victims of the world because I am one. And, most amusingly, I am quite often both at the same time. A long, long time ago it was explained to me that there are no victims in life, only volunteers. Needless to say, I did not understand this statement at the first hearing, but over time the truth of this statement became ever clearer. It also seemed extremely heartless to say there are no victims when so many unfortunates have been brutalized at the hands of mean and vindictive people of every culture, color, and creed. How can there be no victims with such overwhelming evidence to the contrary?

Rather than answering that question head on, this question should lead us back to an earlier question asked in this book: "Who the hell are you?" The truth is, you are what you say you are. For example, have you ever noticed that the people who say they are lucky are always winning stuff? They win door prizes, bingo, and just about every raffle. They believe they are lucky, and they are. Now, you might say, "they say this because it's the truth," and we would agree, but it is also true because they believe it to be true.

Within that last statement is an invitation for you to choose. What is your choice to be: to believe you are lucky because good things happen to you, or to believe good things happen to you because you believe you are lucky? There is a great difference between these two choices, and everything in your life depends upon your choice. And if you have done any research during the reading of this book, you have come a long way in understanding a little about "who the hell you are."

When I was a child, I remember very vividly, my mom would reprimand me and say, "Stop your complaining" or "Stop your bellyaching." I find that last one quite amusing as it would imply there is something wrong with your child if his stomach aches. Anyway, I was a complainer, I really was. I was addicted to it, and I found a host of friends who would accommodate my bellyaching. In fact, they seemed to enjoy it. I had drinking buddies, ministers, and counselors, all more than willing to listen to my endless string of complaints. Even when things were going somewhat well, I would complain about the state of the nation or some cause halfway around the world, some injustice or wrong I would righteously defend. I complained about the weather, my marriage, my kid, sex, no sex, and money. Oh! I loved complaining about money or, rather, the lack of it. It seemed I could never have enough of it. And if I did, I was sure it wouldn't last very long. And I complained about not being lucky and guess what, I wasn't. I lost at just about anything I tried to win. When I say I was a complainer, you can trust me. I have since found out that, when a person complains about anything, they are in fact making themselves a victim, or, at the very least, a martyr (a very polite victim in disguise).

I know you might be thinking that this is not the kind of victim we are talking about, and I would disagree. I have been robbed three times, falsely accused, ripped off, humiliated both privately and publicly, and even beaten up. I have been cheated on romantically repeatedly, and I have lost businesses and filed for bankruptcy. I have unfairly lost friendships and relationships with children because of the unguarded gossip of an ex and yet I am not a victim.

Why am I not a victim in these situations? It is true these things were done to me by others. Yet still I am not a victim because I now know the truth and I know who I am. Here I will introduce a rather difficult concept to wrap your mind around. It's not a very popular one, but it's one that will forever alter your reality for the better if you can accept it. All you need to do is answer one question. Do you want to be a victim? Think long and hard on this. Do not rush to answer. Could there be some kind of payoff for remaining a victim? There is no right or wrong answer, only the truth, and the truth shall set you free.

Most of us continue to play the victim/martyr card long after the crime or perpetration has been enacted. Why? First of all, we may not understand the nature of what just happened. Second, we have forgotten who we are. Third, we hang on because we are getting something out of staying stuck. We are getting an invisible payoff, and there are even times when we secretly relish in identifying with it. I know I did.

"That's absurd!" you might be saying to yourself. What could a person possibly get by playing the victim role? Most of the time it comes down to one answer: sympathy. Yes, sympathy and/or pity, equally bad bedfellows. It is out of our longing to be loved that we play the victim and settle for sympathy. The truth is, it seems to work for the most part. But it is also quite addictive because these two can never fully satisfy and will always leave you wanting more.

Like I say, I was a complainer, a victim, and I know now why I did it. I desperately needed love and had become quite addicted to sympathy and pity instead. I did this for more than half my life. I settled for sympathy when I could have had love all along. I'll tell you how that happened in a bit but first I must tell you how I became a villain as well.

You see, whenever I am complaining, I am acting as a victim—every time. You and I now know that, but what might not be so obvious is that whenever you have a victim, you must have a villain. No exceptions! You cannot have one without the other. This is where it gets very interesting. Read this very slowly. You can't have a victim without a villain, and there may be times when we are perceiving something being done to us when, in actuality, the person/s we have vilified is simply doing this act not to us, but for them. In this scenario, I have just volunteered to be a victim, bought the T-shirt, and signed on the dotted line.

And could it also be that my own self-centeredness is actually the culprit and it has little to nothing to do with the offending party? I know, for myself, that this was exactly the case, countless times, in both of my marriages. When my spouse was simply taking care of herself and it did not jibe with my demands, I played the victim. This is where it gets really unfair because when I chose to be the victim, I inadvertently made them the villain. How unfair is that? Who's the real villain now?

So, if you're like me and you are tired of being or acting like a victim, to my knowledge there is but one way out; you must love yourself out of this. Gone are the days when you could get other people to authentically love you, for you have now trained them too well to just feel sorry for you. No, you must take the lead in this, and this is where you must call upon the knowledge of who you really are. You are the offspring of the creator himself, and there is nothing left but for you to start doing what you needed to do from the beginning. You must begin to LOVE yourself! You must start to give you the care, the attention, and the compassion you desperately crave. You must risk being selfish. If it is selfish to love yourself, then so be it. You won't ever stop being a victim until you do.

It may sound corny, but you can start loving yourself by giving yourself a hug. I mean that literally. When I first was told to do this, I lied to the person who suggested it and said I already do that. I did not want to be that vulnerable and something just felt wrong about it—selfish! When my spiritual advisor noticed I wasn't getting any better in this area, he pushed again for the truth and I came clean and confessed that I had lied and had not actually hugged myself.

He replied, "I know. If you had, you would have changed. It's not until we really learn to genuinely care for ourselves that we let everybody else off the hook. And, paradoxically, when that happens, we end up getting so much more love than we had ever bargained for. Because we are no longer demanding love and trying to manipulate it out of others, people are totally free to love us, with no strings attached. That's the way of it."

He had a way of making sense of things, so I tried it. Then I tried it again and slowly I began, for the first time, to mean it. I started to really care for myself. It really works if done sincerely. And, as an added bonus, I never settled for sympathy ever again. For I am now loved. I don't want you to take my word for it. Try it yourself. Try it repeatedly. One of two things will happen: one, you will feel such overwhelming love and acceptance that you will wonder how you ever survived this long without loving yourself; or two, you will vehemently defend why you just can't do this. Perhaps you might even throw this book away in an attempt to never broach this task again.

You can easily do an acid test on yourself to see if you're really ready to give up your victimization once and for all. And that is this: the next time someone challenges your real or perceived victimization, perhaps being unsympathetic by calling you to accountability, do you find yourself firing back with your own defensive assault? "How dare you! You just don't understand! How could you? I am just ... Just ... Just ... Justifying!" If this is your course, then you will know you are not done yet and you will remain a victim. And that's okay. Really! I mean that! There is only one problem with this type of attitude. We tend to attract what we are.

If, on the other hand, you decide to allow them the dignity of their opinion and simply return to loving yourself, maybe even more, you will know then that you are free, no longer a victim but a VICTOR! And there is one great blessing to this attitude. We tend to attract what we are.

Chapter Eighteen
Warmer, Warmer
Colder, Colder

I have a few grandkids now, and recently I found myself playing a game with my three-year-old granddaughter, the game of warmer, warmer. I hadn't thought of that game for years, like fifty years. A half century! OMG! How'd that happen?

Anyway, this game of warmer, warmer is how we find something hidden. One player hides something in a room or the yard, barn, etc., and as the other player/s try to find the hidden treasure, the host announces loudly if they are getting closer or farther away from the hidden object by saying warmer, warmer or colder, colder. Ultimately the host ends up declaring, "Warmer, warmer, hotter and hotter. You're burning up!" just before a player lays hands on the prize. It's a fun game! I wonder why I ever stopped playing it.

This reminds me of another, similar metaphor. I'm referring to the metaphor or, rather, the other truth I left out at the beginning of this book but promised to get to: "Ask and it shall be given unto you." This fourth universal truth is probably the most misunderstood of all of the truths and none lends itself to runaway, rampant selfishness more than this one. This truth has been witnessed and shared throughout time by many religions and cultures.

As I was growing up hearing "Ask and it shall be given unto

you" read from our Bible, I remember quite vividly wishing for this thing or that, praying, sometimes with great earnestness. Matthew 7:7 actually says, "Ask and it is given; seek and ye shall find; knock and the door shall be opened unto you." Now as a child, I thought I had just found the golden ticket! I prayed and I prayed, yet nothing would happen. I was disappointed, dismayed! Perplexed by my results, I asked my church elders; they were quick to point out my selfishness, saying it didn't work because I was praying for my own selfish ends. But in my ten-year-old mind's defense, if God didn't mean it, then why put something like that into the Bible? Many other well-meaning spiritual teachers in my life pointed out that we had to ask the right way and pray for the right things, for "holy things." This new bit of information didn't help me at all, but it did explain why I wasn't getting what I asked for. I would soon learn to give up on wanting anything ever again.

Except I did want things. I just didn't know it was okay or how to actually get them. Was it as simple as asking? Surely not! Was it just a matter of asking and then working hard? I knew that wasn't true, because I became a very hard worker and still came up short. Was it a matter of knowledge, intelligence, etc.? Over and over again, I had living evidence to the contrary. There had to be something more to the story—that is, if this promise was actually true: *ask and it shall be given unto you.*

When reading this verse again, I noticed something. Most of us have little trouble with *seek and we will find, knock, it will open*, but we do seem to have great difficulty with the *ask and ye shall receive* part. Why is that? I believe, if we were to get really honest with ourselves, it is because we believe that to want or to ask for things from the universe, God, etc., is somehow selfish, that our desire is now tainted or blemished and not PURE. It would seem the very act of asking deems it so. And consequently, many of us remain silent. But, my ten-year-old heart pipes up again, why put this in the Bible if it's not true?

Deciding to dig deeper, I read it again and noticed for the first time that these three statements form one statement. Perhaps the passage's real value isn't as three individual statements but as one collective statement. When looked at in this manner, *ask and it shall be given, seek and ye shall find, knock and the door shall be opened unto you* would appear to be saying that when you engage with the creator, he/she/it engages back.

This, I believe, is probably closer to the true meaning of this verse. And I had never noticed it before now. I am learning so much by writing this book. See! I told you this book was for me! This is where playing the game of warmer, warmer could become very useful, with emphasis on the word *play*. For life is, after all, a game, and we are all meant to PLAY it. What if the universe/God wants in on the game too? What if our role in the game is to seek, knock, and ask, and the universe's job is to call out, "Warmer, warmer, colder, colder, warmer, warmer; you're burning up?" What if?

Chapter Nineteen

Have You Learned Your Lesson Yet?

Do you like that question? Neither do I! In fact, I have never liked that question, and I cringe at the thought of ever asking it to another human being, although I have done exactly that, especially when it came to children. That was also when I first heard this question. I was a child and I was being punished for some transgression that I probably, in all honesty, did commit.

But this statement has much greater implications for our lives than we might see at first glance. For instance, how many times have you heard someone stating that this or that is a test of their faith, or that there was a lesson in this or that experience? Or even quite boldly stating that God is teaching us a lesson? How many of us believe that life is just a series of tests to see who's worthy to go on? To graduate, so to speak, to a higher level of consciousness—to heaven? Maybe it's a pass/fail kind of thing, or maybe there are differing states of nirvana. What is the meaning of life, really?

Do I believe a supreme being created us out of himself? If this were true, then what would be the purpose of a piece of God proving to the all-knowing God that it is, after all, worthy? This would be an absurd test, wouldn't you agree? Wouldn't the creator recognize a piece of himself? Would it benefit God to cast himself into outer darkness? What would be the sense in that? Do I still believe in a judgmental and condemning God?

If, however, God is not judgmental or condemning and is in

fact pure LOVE, then what is the purpose of life? If we are already loved and it's not about deserving the love or approval of a higher power but is in fact a love that is unconditional, then wherein lies the purpose of all this? All this struggle, all this challenge, all this suffering? What could possibly be the point?

When I was a kid, I spent hours and hours playing tic-tac-toe. I would do this because my older brother (five years older) would beat me at the game every time. I was determined to win at least once, so I kept trying. An interesting thing happened. The older I got, the more I started to win. Then came the day I found out that the game is rigged. Once you understand the game completely, it is only a matter of who goes first that determines who will win.

Needless to say, the game quickly became boring and I moved on to more challenging pursuits. But I can't deny the fun of all those years I loved playing the game in the hope of beating my brother. My brother, on the other hand, never let on that the game was rigged. I think he enjoyed winning a little too much! And there was an added benefit to learning the tricks of tic-tac-toe. I could beat my younger sister every time. Knowledge is a powerful thing!

Back to my question. What's the point of all this (life) if it's not a test to see who gets to pass Go and collect $200 (Monopoly, another favorite game)? Are we, like so many believe, learning lessons so we can graduate to higher levels of consciousness? Is that what I am supposed to believe? If that is the case, I seem to have been held back a few grades. I also don't understand how you could ever be tested for something you were not ever given the chance to study for.

Does this "life is a test" argument hold up under examination? Does this jibe with the notion of an all-powerful and loving creator caring unconditionally about our lives and what we experience here on earth? What would be the purpose of intentionally holding some of us back while others appear to be graduating with honors? Isn't it obvious that there are those who are simply born into better environments and families, taught better skills? All of this results in a noticeably better life. If there is a loving creator and if it is true that we are here to learn lessons, then it sure appears that God plays favorites. It seems obvious that there are teacher's pets, people who butter up the teacher, play by all the rules, and get a gold star at the end of the day. Could this be what life is about, just playing by the rules? Could it be that only a lucky few get to have their names written on the honor list as the rest of us unfortunates sit in the corner donning our stylish but outdated dunce hats?

No!!!! It seems obvious that something is severely wrong with this model of reality if we do believe in a creator that really loves and cares about each and every one of us and stands ever ready to assist if we solicit his help. Yes, there must be more to the equation than this. This is the spot I came to and it's a helluva spot at that! My previous model of a higher power and everything it entails (that God loved me, BUT ... fill in the blank) wasn't working for me at all. In fact, it nearly killed me! The futility of believing in that kind of a God—that no matter what I did, I would be left unworthy of love, ever wanting of the peace promised me—had me by the throat, strangling the very life essence out of me. I had to question this belief that I must perform well if I was to earn God's grace, that only if I believe a certain way, be baptized the "right" way, and admit my unworthiness, then and only then would I pass the test, then and only then may I spend eternity with my creator in everlasting bliss. But in the meantime, I must SUFFER!

I could no longer subscribe to this belief for if my creator really did love me, then it just didn't make sense that I should have to somehow earn his love. I had to find another purpose for living, for life. If life isn't a test and we do not need to earn God's love and are indeed loved unconditionally—there are no favorites, no brownie points—then what could possibly be the purpose in all this? Or is there no purpose, after all? That doesn't make me feel very good! Even if that were the case, my life is better not believing such a notion.

Furthermore, if life isn't a test, and it isn't supposed to be hard and challenging, then is life supposed to be easy? Are we meant to live on Easy Street, standing in line occasionally with hands out, as our creator does all the hard work and divvies out our blessings, unearned and probably unappreciated (as that seems to always be the case with people once they get used to handouts).

Is life easy, without challenge, without struggle? Life itself appears to laugh audibly at such a notion. This notion has nothing if not overwhelming evidence to the contrary. No, this certainly cannot be true. So what could possibly be the meaning of life?

What could possibly be left? What could possibly be our choice? Do we have a choice? Of course, we do! And here is the only choice that appears to make any sense to me.

Life is not supposed to be easy! Life is not supposed to be hard. Life is meant to be FUN!

Life is meant to be FUN! ADVENTUROUS, CREATIVE, EXCITING, and WORTHWHILE! It's about the adventure of it all, the creation of it all, both the good and the bad, the not knowing. Another word for fun is JOY! It is a JOY to be challenged! It's exciting! It is the anticipation of not knowing if I am going to win at checkers. If games didn't have an element of chance, they would hold no lasting interest to us. If LIFE had no element of chance, it would also be of no real interest to us. You know it and I know it.

Learning a new skill is exciting. Even struggle can have its rewards for us. It is WORTHWHILE to go through something so hard that it nearly takes your breath away, literally, only to come out the other side with a message of hope so powerful that it changes for the better the lives of all those walking behind us. It is a JOY to be a leader, a follower, a bystander. Life is the GAME and is meant to be enjoyed, IN JOYED!!

Those who do not agree are simply caught in the all-too-familiar trap of taking life too seriously, like the golfer playing the game of golf and getting so wrapped up in the winning/losing aspect that he throws his golf clubs into the pond after a failed putt. Silly, just plain silly!

And as with any game, winning or losing is just the opportunity to experience fully the different emotions of opposite outcomes. The true value of any game is not in winning or losing, but in the thrill experienced in the playing of it. We were meant to PLAY this game called life! It's all in our attitudes toward life that determine whether we will actually enjoy the game. When you make the game of life about winning or losing, you will surely lose every time. You've heard it said that the joy is in the journey. Well, the joy is in the PLAYING of the GAME.

You're in the game anyway. You're already out there on the field, suited up; there are no bench sitters, there are no second stringers. The ball is being thrown to you, so you might as well enjoy it. Give it a shot. Play the game. What have you got to lose? Ultimately there is nothing more worthwhile than the JOY of loving and being loved! There is no greater experience than to have once lived in darkness, pain, suffering, despair, and longing, and from that dark and lonely place to come into the blinding light of the awareness of unconditional love. This transformation of going from night to day is an experience so profound that all other human experiences pale in comparison. When we come into the deep and powerful knowing of this truth, our lives are forever changed and we experience for the first time the usefulness of all those so-called bad experiences. Having survived, we now have the opportunity to put them, all of them, to good use.

Why? Because the pinnacle of human achievement is not the mountaintop experience of spiritual transformation but the humbling service we offer others when we tell our very personal message of deliverance to receptive ears, to watch others "get it," to watch them have their own AHA moments as they blossom into new lives. Share in these events; you will not want to miss it! It is wildly exciting! It's intoxicatingly worthwhile! It is adventuresome and thrilling, and I hope you are selfish enough to seek this extraordinary experience. There is no greater way to live! There is no greater way to LOVE!

Chapter Twenty
The Workout

"How selfish is that? They decided to work out at the gym again and did not consider my feelings at all. I wanted to spend time with them and all they can think about is getting healthy, they are sooooo SELFISH!"

You may think this statement is a ridiculous example of selfishness, and you would be right. It is ridiculous, but, if we are being honest, we must admit that there have been numerous times when we have done exactly this but under different circumstances. I hope you can identify the real selfish individual in this opening statement. How many times do we inadvertently point our boney fingers at others and decide their guilt and selfishness and haven't got a clue as to our own? I suspect it is much more often than we would care to acknowledge. I would hope you can agree with me on this, as that means there is hope for us after all. If you can't or have never seen your own selfishness, then you are either a saint or beyond help. But, if you can admit that you have, on occasion, taken the lofty high road and sat in judgment of another's intent, then join the club, the "health club" of selfish bastards. Your membership will last a lifetime and you will never lose your benefits.

What better example than the gym to illustrate that selfish acts can be a very healthy thing? And there is something you should know about working out; if you work out for someone else, it probably won't work out. However, working out tends to work just fine when you work out for yourself. Working out for yourself does also have its benefits for those close to you. But watching other people work out will not make you fit. You will have to do that for yourself. Only the person working out gets fit, feels better and healthier, and lives longer. They not only get fit; they get sexier and have more energy. Yeah!

But even though other individuals might not get direct benefit from someone else working out, they do get to enjoy those benefits secondhand. They get to be inspired to get healthy too. They get to admire those dedicated to working out! They like what working out does to the body. They like looking at the results. And if two people in a relationship are working out together, all the better. This single act can be quite an elixir of life and love, unless, of course, you're working out AT someone.

All of this proves my point: if you are making time for yourself to exercise, you are practicing self-love and you are benefiting yourself mostly, which means this act falls under the exact definition of selfishness. Crazy, isn't it? You cannot deny that it is a selfish act, but if you're anything like me, you may be wanting to scream out, "But that's different!" But is it? Really?

What better example to illustrate my point? Many of us are judged selfish, but few deeds indeed are entirely or completely selfish acts. What may look like selfishness on the surface may simply be us following what we believe to be in our best interest. Like when we are working out, we think we will benefit from this action. Keep in mind that there is no private good. Not only do we benefit by our decision to do what's best for us, but frequently others benefit as well. Then there are those who sit on the sidelines and condemn the actions of others and consequently reap little if any benefit. They are usually individuals with their own agenda and may actually prove to be the selfish ones after all.

Now, I know there are plenty of selfish acts out there and plenty of selfish people, but if I were to draw some sort of conclusion, it would be this. I am not the best person to decide what is selfish or not for anyone else other than myself. I will leave that task to those more qualified, the saints. And if you're one of those "perfect" people, then more power to you! I'll just worry about myself and take care of keeping my own magic carpet clean. I will decide if I am selfish or selfless, perhaps maybe even drop the question altogether and just BE a BE-ing. Is that selfish? You betcha! Is that self-ish? You betcha! Is that divine? You betcha!

Chapter Twenty-One

It's about Happy

The Ultimate Selfish Act

"How dare you be happy? Don't you see how miserable I am, how I am suffering?" How many of us have thought this when we were going through something particularly difficult and some smiling jerk comes into our space and tries to cast a pleasant rainbow about our dark and dismal room with his or her sunny disposition? How many of us have actually said something like this? Isn't it common for us to think it is somehow RUDE to be happy when others are not? Don't we secretly or openly feel that if someone is suffering, we must approach these poor souls with long faces and sympathetic and sorrowful eyes full of pity and empathy? How many of us choose to be happy in the presence of suffering? How many of us feel the pangs of fearful retaliation for such social improprieties? How many of us are too scared to offer sufferers what they actually need in lieu of what they want to hear? How many of us are conflicted when it comes to what we want to do and what we should do when faced with these occurrences? How many of us have an answer at hand, a solution to what ails the sufferer, but we opt to lend sympathy instead? Are we correct in keeping our mouths shut? Are we allowed to be happy in the presence of suffering? Is it right to be? Will we just be adding insult to injury? Do we really know what to do in these sometimes-awkward situations, or are we still under the false illusion that sympathy actually makes suffering people feel better? Does it? Does sympathy really help, or do we inadvertently heap additional layers of pity to the already suffering person? Why is it so natural to offer sympathy? How many of us confuse sympathy for love? How many of us feel that we must be sympathetic or otherwise we would be a heartless monster?

I'm here to tell you that sympathy is a very poor substitute for true compassion. True compassion is relieving a person's suffering, not adding to it. In case I'm confusing you a bit, let me tell you a very personal story about how I was a very sympathetic soul and how addicted I was to sympathy myself. And just like any addiction, once you get some, it's never enough and will always leave you wanting more.

When I was a child, a young boy in a very large family, it was very common to get lost in the shuffle, so to speak. I remember vividly waiting my turn to sit on my mother's lap. I must have been all but four years old. My younger sister, maybe eighteen months old, seemed to me to be hogging all my mother's attention. I chuckle at my misconception now. I was a baby jealous of a baby!

I have a granddaughter now, and my behavior all those years ago appears to be not that uncommon, as I can watch my nearly four-year-old granddaughter stand jealously by while her eight-month-old little sister appears to be stealing everybody's attention. It is quite amusing, to say the least, to remember the very same scenario and now see it from an entirely different perspective.

I was so sure of my unimportance as a young lad that I would often throw amazing temper tantrums for attention or to get my way, theatrical performances with a well-choreographed routine. I would yell and scream, flail my arms about like a broken windmill, and, for a finale, thrust myself to the floor, making sure all in the room noticed my gross injustice, followed immediately by a rather prolonged death sequence not dissimilar to the dying swan of *Swan Lake*.

Needless to say, a standing ovation was out of the question and soon I was to come into swift connection with the long arm of the law. I was punished. And if that punishment was for me to be sent to my room, I would end my debut with a well-pronounced lower lip pushed far beyond its normal demur setting, and I would announce my objectionable retreat to my room with very loud stomps up the fifteen or so wooden steps, each one getting louder as I approached the summit. Often I would be called back down the stairs only to repeat my ascent in a quieter manner.

I felt neglected. I'm not saying it was true, but I often felt left out, overlooked, and unimportant. We had seven kids in my family. SEVEN!!! My dad often worked two jobs to support all of us and my mother. God bless my mother; she had to deal with all seven of us, usually at the same time. I was not neglected at all. In fact, I was LOVED very much. But I didn't think so at the time. All I could see was my infant sister getting what should be my attention. Life is so unfair!

Anyway, amid the obvious lack of parental empathy and attention, there were times when I had my mother all to myself. There were times when all seven of us got that beautiful experience of solitary compassion and 100 percent devotion to our needs, and that was when one of us was sick or injured. I remember vividly Mom getting out the very cool metal (I wish they still made those) Band-Aid tin and blowing on my owie before gently applying the bandage. Then she would tenderly kiss my boo-boo (which, by the way, always hurt more) and say, "All better." She was a great mom, an incredible mom. How she ever managed seven of us is beyond me. But because of my experience as a very young child, I started making the erroneous connection between love and sympathy. Whereas love may sometimes include sympathy, sympathy does not always include love and sometimes can actually be the opposite.

Fast-forward a few decades, and as I was going through my greatest personal crisis, I was faced with the realization that I had found myself in a death waltz of my own design. Much like the temper tantrums of my early childhood, my constant demands that life perform for me, line up my way and only my way, this constant need for attention and approval and validation had left me writhing on the floor in agonizing loneliness and confusion. My best had bested me and I was bankrupt. I had nothing left.

That is when I reached out for help and I got it. I really do believe that when a student is ready to change, the teacher, the guru, the God-sent will appear. And much to my dismay, he didn't say what I wanted to hear. He didn't do what I wanted him to do; he would not wallow in my self-pity with me. Instead he told me that sympathy would kill me and that I did not need one more person feeling sorry for me. He went one step further and said something that has stayed with me for more than twenty-five years. "That's why, in the dictionary, the word *sympathy* is between the words *shit* and *syphilis*. And it's just about as worthless."

Now, I have since learned many ways to be compassionate and understanding, but what I have taken away from all these years of experience, all my personal temper tantrums, my hurt, my pain, is that when I am indulging in self-pity, the last thing I ever need is sympathy. I may not want anything else, but if you really care for me, you will offer me a solution instead. Which just so happens to be in the dictionary between *shit* and *syphilis* as well.

Chapter Twenty-Two

Get over Yourself

(It's a Mind Game)

You selfish bastard! By now you may be wondering just how does someone move past being a selfish bastard? How does someone get over himself or herself and become a somewhat less selfish person, even a selfless person? Is there hope for us, the selfish bastards of the world? Actually there is, and it starts with a little stock taking. I think it's important to note that a truly selfish person, someone who is totally wrapped up in the self and quite narcissistic, would probably not have picked up this book in the first place. You may have purchased this book for them or thought that that special selfish someone should really read this book, but I bet they would not probably purchase this book on their own, let alone manage to read to the end. No, I would venture to say this type of person is pretty much convinced there is simply nothing at all wrong with them. There are these types of people in this world, but you are probably not one of them. These truly selfish twits really are quite rare, but they serve a tremendous purpose to the rest of us occupying this little blue ball of ours.

What purpose could that possibly be? They serve a vital role in the dramas of life. They provide contrast and opportunity. They afford us the opportunity to experience something quite divine— tolerance! Yes, tolerance, and sometimes humor. That is, if we haven't fallen into the trap of taking all of this (*life*) too seriously.

You see, without intolerable people we cannot experience tolerance. Without truly self-absorbed, selfish, and self-centered people, we would not experience selflessness.

You may object. *What? How can that possibly be? First you call us selfish bastards and then you say we can't experience true selflessness unless we become tolerant of selfish bastards.* Some of you may even think me a bit touched in the head to even propose such a thing. In my defense, let me start by pointing out something rather obvious: if there were not a need for the selfish bastards of the world, there simply would not be any. That is, unless you think that somehow the universe made a big mistake in creating these unlovable creatures. No, I believe because there most certainly are these types of people, that there must be a purpose for their being, living among us, testing us. There must be a divine purpose; otherwise, we have a creator that has surely lost control of this whole experiment we call life.

I am sure there must be a purpose to all things. Why and how can I believe this? Quite simply put, it makes me feel better to believe this than to not. It costs nothing more to have faith, but it can cost quite a bit more to not have faith. Lack of faith leads to hopelessness and hopelessness reaps a terrible price from the soul. So, if you can make the leap that everybody here on earth serves a purpose, a divine calling, then it's not such a big step to understand that some things, some people, are going to be harder to understand than others. There are people who are easy to love, then there are the difficult ones, and finally the downright unlovable, right? We see examples of this every day, and, if you're like me, the last thing you would ever want to do (at least not willingly) is to offer one of these unsightly and unlovable beings something they do not deserve. No, I would much rather give them exactly what they deserve, if you know what I mean.

There are a few of us, however, who may think we are quite tolerant of people and their "unlovableness"—that is, until they directly affect us with their selfishness and self-centeredness. Then it's a different story. For now, we have good reason to not love or tolerate them and we may even feel quite justified in retaliating. But giving these creatures what they *do not* deserve is actually what is called for here. For without offering the opposite of what is presented us, nothing can be gained by either the unlovable person or ourselves. By simply responding in like manner, tit for tat, so to speak, a huge opportunity to experience the divine is missed. We have lost the opportunity to become selfless and thus remain selfish bastards ourselves. Loving the unlovable may seem quite an order and, probably for most, an impossible task, and that is where tolerance comes in. Tolerance does not ask us to feel good about the selfish person in question, but rather that we allow them their divine right to BE as they are. Tolerance thus becomes the bridge for the unlovable to reach the shores of love. Often tolerance is the closest thing unlovables experience to love, and without tolerance, most unlovables would truly be hopeless.

Like we discovered in a previous chapter, if your purpose is to be a nurse or a doctor or some kind of healer, then you're going to need sick people. If you want to be a social worker, a psychiatrist, or someone who works in mental health, then you're going to need people who aren't quite right in the head and you're going to need plenty of them. Otherwise, you'll never have a career. If you want to build houses or fix things, then you're going to need things that break, wear down, and fall apart. It doesn't matter what you want to be or become, the opposite of what you want to contribute will have to show up first. You have to have a need to fill before you can fill it. And here is where these selfish bastards line up backstage waiting for their cues. They are creating a need. They are simply playing their part so you can play your part of being tolerant, loving, and kind. Selfless.

It's one thing to be selfless with people you love, people who depend on you, or people who treat you somewhat nicely, at least some of the time, and it's quite another thing to be selfless in the presence of a selfish bastard. To find a place of compassion with these special messengers is a journey you will not want to miss. The love and tolerance needed to forbear these devilish angels is truly transformative and can help you get over your own narcissism and selfishness. After all, isn't it us who picked up this book in the first place? Shouldn't we of all people understand the narcissist? Don't we know firsthand what it's like to think only of ourselves? Weren't we just moments ago asking for love and tolerance and understanding? Didn't we buy this book in the hope of getting over our own selfishness? Finally, if we are intolerant of the intolerable, then why should anyone ever tolerate us? Wouldn't we be asking others to do what we ourselves are unwilling to do?

After it's all said and done, I think I will ask you to try one last game, a mind game. The next time you find yourself judging someone or happen to notice someone else wrapped up in themselves and being a real selfish bastard, if you mentally Photoshop your own face onto theirs, your own mind into theirs, it would go a long way in transforming the problem of selfishness into the solution of selflessness. This person has given you a great opportunity to demonstrate exactly what you would love to be, the highest version of you: a SELFLESS BLESSING. A very wise man once said, "When you do it unto the least of these [wonder who he's talking about?] you do it unto me." After all, in the big scope of things, we are one!

About the Author

D. Arthur just may be a Selfish Bastard, but then again, it takes one to know one!

Humorously crafted and superbly executed, Wilson's enticing narrative examines the human condition while it observes the human condition. The pages engage the reader and takes them on an unexpected journey... a journey into themselves... ourselves.

D. Arthur likes to joke that he is an expert in the field of behavior and believes himself always to be behaving... just sometimes badly! Wilson offers wit and wisdom earned from the school of Hard Knox and humorously poses profound questions that are sure to penetrate the hearts and minds of the readers searching to find answers about those selfish bastards in their lives and what in the world to do with them. Even if "we" are the "them".

A celebrated Professional Artist for over four decades with installations and collectors worldwide, Wilson's latest art form is with pen and paper... words. D. Arthur was gifted with a world-wide pandemic, plenty of time on his hands and even a shattered collar bone to boot. All these circumstances came together to provide D. Arthur with the necessary time and motivation to write his inaugural self-help book. Or at least, it took away all his excuses.

Wilson shares life with his gorgeous wife Lisa, four phenomenal sons, daughters-in-law, a wonderful mother-in-law and four amazing granddaughters, all of which he selfishly adores.

Other Books by Ozark Mountain Publishing, Inc.

Dolores Cannon
A Soul Remembers Hiroshima
Between Death and Life
Conversations with Nostradamus,
    Volume I, II, III
The Convoluted Universe -Book One,
    Two, Three, Four, Five
The Custodians
Five Lives Remembered
Horns of the Goddess
Jesus and the Essenes
Keepers of the Garden
Legacy from the Stars
The Legend of Starcrash
The Search for Hidden Sacred
    Knowledge
They Walked with Jesus
The Three Waves of Volunteers and the
    New Earth
A Very Special Friend
Aron Abrahamsen
Holiday in Heaven
James Ream Adams
Little Steps
Justine Alessi & M. E. McMillan
Rebirth of the Oracle
Kathryn Andries
Time: The Second Secret
Will Alexander
Call Me Jonah
Cat Baldwin
Divine Gifts of Healing
The Forgiveness Workshop
Penny Barron
The Oracle of UR
P.E. Berg & Amanda Hemmingsen
The Birthmark Scar
Dan Bird
Finding Your Way in the Spiritual Age
Waking Up in the Spiritual Age
Julia Cannon
Soul Speak – The Language of Your
    Body
Jack Cauley
Journey for Life
Ronald Chapman
Seeing True
Jack Churchward
Lifting the Veil on the Lost
    Continent of Mu

The Stone Tablets of Mu
Carolyn Greer Daly
Opening to Fullness of Spirit
Patrick De Haan
The Alien Handbook
Paulinne Delcour-Min
Divine Fire
Holly Ice
Spiritual Gold
Anthony DeNino
The Power of Giving and Gratitude
Joanne DiMaggio
Edgar Cayce and the Unfulfilled
    Destiny of Thomas Jefferson
    Reborn
Paul Fisher
Like a River to the Sea
Anita Holmes
Twidders
Aaron Hoopes
Reconnecting to the Earth
Edin Huskovic
God is a Woman
Patricia Irvine
In Light and In Shade
Kevin Killen
Ghosts and Me
Susan Linville
Blessings from Agnes
Donna Lynn
From Fear to Love
Curt Melliger
Heaven Here on Earth
Where the Weeds Grow
Henry Michaelson
And Jesus Said – A Conversation
Andy Myers
Not Your Average Angel Book
Holly Nadler
The Hobo Diaries
Guy Needler
The Anne Dialogues
Avoiding Karma
Beyond the Source – Book 1, Book 2
The Curators
The History of God
The OM
The Origin Speaks

For more information about any of the above titles, soon to be released titles,
or other items in our catalog, write, phone or visit our website:
PO Box 754, Huntsville, AR 72740|479-738-2348/800-935-0045|www.ozarkmt.com

Other Books by Ozark Mountain Publishing, Inc.

Psycho Spiritual Healing
James Nussbaumer
And Then I Knew My Abundance
Each of You
Living Your Dram, Not Someone Else's
The Master of Everything
Mastering Your Own Spiritual Freedom
Sherry O'Brian
Peaks and Valley's
Gabrielle Orr
Akashic Records: One True Love
Let Miracles Happen
Nikki Pattillo
Children of the Stars
A Golden Compass
Victoria Pendragon
Being In A Body
Sleep Magic
The Sleeping Phoenix
Alexander Quinn
Starseeds What's It All About
Debra Rayburn
Let's Get Natural with Herbs
Charmian Redwood
A New Earth Rising
Coming Home to Lemuria
Richard Rowe
Exploring the Divine Library
Imagining the Unimaginable
Garnet Schulhauser
Dance of Eternal Rapture
Dance of Heavenly Bliss
Dancing Forever with Spirit
Dancing on a Stamp
Dancing with Angels in Heaven
Annie Stillwater Gray
The Dawn Book
Education of a Guardian Angel
Joys of a Guardian Angel
Work of a Guardian Angel
Manuella Stoerzer
Headless Chicken

Blair Styra
Don't Change the Channel
Who Catharted
Natalie Sudman
Application of Impossible Things
L.R. Sumpter
Judy's Story
The Old is New
We Are the Creators
Artur Tradevosyan
Croton
Croton II
Jim Thomas
Tales from the Trance
Jolene and Jason Tierney
A Quest of Transcendence
Paul Travers
Dancing with the Mountains
Nicholas Vesey
Living the Life-Force
Dennis Wheatley/ Maria Wheatley
The Essential Dowsing Guide
Maria Wheatley
Druidic Soul Star Astrology
Sherry Wilde
The Forgotten Promise
Lyn Willmott
A Small Book of Comfort
Beyond all Boundaries Book 1
Beyond all Boundaries Book 2
Beyond all Boundaries Book 3
D. Arthur Wilson
You Selfish Bastard
Stuart Wilson & Joanna Prentis
Atlantis and the New Consciousness
Beyond Limitations
The Essenes -Children of the Light
The Magdalene Version
Power of the Magdalene
Sally Wolf
Life of a Military Psychologist

For more information about any of the above titles, soon to be released titles,
or other items in our catalog, write, phone or visit our website:
PO Box 754, Huntsville, AR 72740|479-738-2348/800-935-0045|www.ozarkmt.com